MANAGEMENT DECISION-MAKING

Management Series

MANAGEMENT DECISION-MAKING

PROF. WILLIAM T. MORRIS
PROF. HAROLD BIERMAN
PROF. GEORGE A. TAYLOR
DR R. A. CUNINGHAME-GREEN
DR DAVID A. COUTS

A PAN ORIGINAL

Introduced and Edited by
GORDON A. YEWDALL

PAN BOOKS LTD · LONDON

First published 1969 by Pan Books Ltd.,
33 Tothill Street, London, S.W.1.

ISBN 0 330 02225 3

2nd Printing 1972

Printed in Great Britain by
Cox & Wyman Ltd., London, Reading and Fakenham

CONTENTS

Page

INTRODUCTION   *Gordon A. Yewdall*   xi

PART I

MANAGEMENT DECISIONS – ART OR SCIENCE?
William T. Morris   1

Chapter

1. Framing the Question   3
   Historical Versions of the Question – Modern Versions of the Question

2. Art as Intuition   9

3. A Model of the Management-Decision Process   13

4. Analysing the Decision Process   17
   Selectivity and Simplification – Need-Determined Distortions – Learning

5. The Uses of Science   22
   Predicting Policy Consequences – Learning from Experience

6. Management as Experiment   29
   Explicit Method – Experiment and Experience – Uses of Intuition – Pressure of Affairs – The Basic Proposal

PART II

QUANTITATIVE DECISION-MAKING
Harold Bierman, Jr.   37

7. The Nature of Decision-Making   41

8. The Future of Quantitative Decision-Making   53
   Development of Mathematical Models – Decision Theory – Example

9. A Technical Note on Uncertainty 63
   *Decision-Making with Uncertainty where Time is
   a Factor – Solutions Correct and Incorrect – A
   Single Lottery – Conclusion*

PART III

THE FOUNDATIONS OF THE INVESTMENT
DECISION *George A. Taylor* 73

10. The Executive Roles of the Businessman 75
    *The Businessman's Awareness – Executive Roles –
    The Most Difficult Role – Creative Thinking –
    Decision-Making – Economics – Qualitative Tests
    – Satisfaction – Improving Creative Abilities –
    Quantitative Tests*

11. Making Investment Decisions 87
    *Types of Spending Decisions – Investments –
    Examples – Alternatives – Criteria for Spending
    Decisions – Cost of Capital – Cutoff Rate –
    Evaluating the Spending Decision – Other Factors*

12. Evaluation Methods Evaluated 98
    *Some Popular Methods – Squeaky Wheel Tech-
    nique – Necessity Technique – Payout Method*

13. Why Science? The Final Reasons and
    Responsibilities 105
    *Essential Reasons for Scientifically Analysing
    Spending Decisions – Responsibility for the
    Analysis of Spending Decisions – Conclusion*

PART IV

THE STOCK DECISION *R. A. Cuninghame-Green* 111

14. Once upon a Time 113
    *The Once-only Problem – Complexity of Con-
    sequence – Diversity of Criteria – Value of
    Information*

15. The Recurrent Decision 121
    *Time Series – Routine Stock Planning – Exponen-
    tial Smoothing – Properties of the Index – The
    Seasonal Product – Summary*

16. Additional Complexities   137
     *Top-up Systems – Lead Time – Emergency Orders
     – (S,s) and EO Q – Multi-item case – Interacting
     Items – The Manufacturer's Problem*

17. Mathematical Appendix   148
     *Exponential Smoothing – General Exponential
     Smoothing – Relative Demand Distribution –
     Policy Stock – Economic Order Quantity –
     Distributor's Problem*

                    PART V

MATHEMATICAL AND STATISTICAL
FORECASTING   *David A. Couts*   153

18. What is Forecasting?   155
     Forecasting Accuracy

19. Operational Approach to Forecasting   158
     *Decision Theory–Classical Statistics – Elementary
     Statistical Concepts*

20. Approaches to Forecasting   165
     Forecasting Models – Formal and Structural

21. Statistical Techniques of Forecasting   171
     *Forecasting Procedures – Regression – Auto-
     regressive Forecasting – Adaptive Forecasting –
     The Implicit Model – Multiple Regression*

22. Examples of Mathematical and Statistical
    Forecasting in Business   193
     *Stock Control – Forecasting Accuracy – Style
     Items – Agricultural Commodities – Mathematical
     Models – Demand for New Product – Canal Tolls*

Preface

As editor, I am grateful to record that the authors presented their contributions in first-class order and required minimal editorial effort. The customary editorial exhortations and onerous fulminations were thereby pleasantly absent in this case, though I do of course accept the usual full responsibility for any errors.

It should be understood almost without saying that all the views expressed in this book are personal to the writers and not necessarily those of the organizations by which they are employed.

Gordon Yewdall

Marlow-on-Thames.
January 1969.

Biographical Note

Gordon Yewdall has lectured and written on statistics and operational research in addition to working as a management consultant. He is at present a principal research officer with the Engineering Industry Training Board. He was secretary of the Capital Investment Group and is now chairman of the Cost Effectiveness Group of the Operational Research Society. He is a member of the Society of Investment Analysts.

INTRODUCTION

The background

More than a dozen books have now appeared in the Pan/Ealing series on Management and it is appropriate to give some explanation of the underlying philosophy of this series. The increasing interest in management studies requires books which are not too specialist but intended for general information; to introduce new students to the subject and to refurbish experienced managers' knowledge by bringing them abreast of recent developments. The method chosen to suit the audience for the series is by providing a comprehensive coverage of the many facets of management paying particular attention to current thinking but nevertheless presenting it in a readable and non-technical manner. The Editorial Advisers have therefore adopted the policy of selecting classical works on management where they cover valuable ground in a suitable manner. Such writers as Peter Drucker, Harold Norcross and Rosemary Stewart bear evidence to the success of this policy.

In addition, the Editorial Advisers have commissioned new books to deal with those topics which break fresh ground. Two recent examples of this policy are the work by D. R. C. Halford on corporate planning, and that by J. J. Lynch on manpower budgeting. Both writers found it necessary to approach management problems by devising new thinking and it is generally agreed that they have made useful contributions to the development of a readable literature on management studies.

Perhaps the most critical 'new' area of contemporary management interest, however, is that embraced by the description 'Management Science'. This area contains mathematical techniques which are now of key importance in management development and includes the application of such studies as statistics, mathematics, computing, operational research and econometrics – a collection of disciplines guaranteed to make for tough reading by any non-numerate manager. The techniques involved are much beyond the necessary scientific background experience of the average manager, largely perhaps as a result of the short-sighted educational policies which lead to a high level of premature specialization in schools and colleges, thereby ensuring that the arts side is not contaminated in any useful way by contacts with science or mathematics. The sins of too early specialization bear their largest fruits in Britain when the arts men who become managers find their need for some understanding of scientific disciplines too often increases in direct proportion to their lack of knowledge about them.

This relationship has already encouraged a multitude of writers to attempt to deal with various aspects of the disciplines together with their management applications. Such studies have been relatively unsuccessful, however, for one chief reason – the writers have generally failed to appreciate the manager's capability and requirement for mathematical thought. This is evidenced by the large number of books which contain in their sub-titles and introductions the phrase 'suitable for the non-mathematical beginner', and then proceed to roll out such a profusion of equations and formulae that the cynical reader might be inclined to assume that the pious prelude was some sort of absolution guaranteed to excuse the writer from the assault he was about to commit in going far beyond the most distant fringes of the average manager's mathematical understanding. Well might the non-numerate manager react by believing that mathematical thinking is only to be understood by persons with 'a peculiar, and regrettably impractical, twist of mind'.

As far as the average manager is concerned, therefore, mathematical wizardry is divorced from practical competence, to such an extent that one might paraphrase the belief of Sir Paul Chambers that it is only the exceptional mathematician who is strong enough to rise above the natural inclinations of his mathematical education and make his way in business. What is clearly needed to bridge this management numeracy gap is a series of texts which emphasize the logical analysis of problem structures coupled with a quantitive approach and an insight into computer utilization – as distinct from texts which become frighteningly advanced in their attempts to *retrain* the manager in patterns of mathematical thinking. It is the intention of this book to emphasize the logical structures of management activity. The structures are established by William Morris and George Taylor, while the quantitive approach is developed by Hal Bierman and Ray Cuninghame-Green, and the insight into computer forecasting is given by David Couts

The problem of who should write a book on management science is inextricably linked with the content matter since failure to communicate with the audience means a complete waste of effort irrespective of the beauty of theories. This is not to imply that the content should be so naïve that the book becomes reduced to a collection of obvious platitudes and trite generalizations. The value of a good text is that it combines the virtues of presenting a moderate intellectual challenge and opening new vistas in the reader's mind so that the experienced manager is able to say 'Yes, indeed, this has an important message for me within the ambit of my own activity'.

In order to ensure the practical value of such a book we have invited contributions only from experienced writers who were international experts in their subject and whose previous writings indicated that they would ideally be able to direct their efforts in a practical presentation to the appropriate level of challenge required by their potential audience. It is in fact extremely rare that one has the opportunity to read the views of such a group of world experts on management science collected side by side. The names of William Morris, Hal Bierman and George Taylor are household words in the realms of management training. And if Ray Cuninghame-Green and David Couts are referred to in one's second breath it is not because they are less capable, but merely that they represent a younger generation than their co-authors. The Pan/Ealing series is indeed fortunate to have such a group of Anglo-American experts to combine their ideas on the hitherto difficult and mystical area of management science.

Management Science and Management Decisions

One should begin by accepting forthwith that there is no such thing as 'scientific management'. There is good management, and there is bad management. The difference between the two is one of complacency. The good manager senses that all is not well, may be able to define his problems, and can thus seek to solve them; a situation which has led R. G. Brown to observe, 'It is more important to state the right problem than to solve it'.

The bad manager is not usually aware of his objectives, let alone his problems. He himself is an object of pity and contempt for he has the invidious task of keeping alert subordinates in check lest their superior knowledge will lead to his replacement. He is unable to delegate responsibilities or to develop suitable organizational structures, or to recruit and keep good supporting management, or to plan ahead effectively, or to adapt to technical and market change, or to show any inspirational commercial leadership of any sort.

The theory of management by 'experience' has been drawn up to keep him in being. This theory rests on the supposition that some mystical 'insight' attaches to the manager's person and this insight can only be developed and matured through many years of experience in the job. Perhaps the cynical observer might believe 'hindsight' were a more apposite and euphemistic description, for whatever judgement this type of manager offers, it always rests upon seat-of-the-pants decisions. The truth is that this theory of management is used to cover up human ignorance, ageing intellectual incompetence, and fear of the natural conclusions that must follow from being required to work with a positive objective. Fortunately, managers of this sort are on the wane, though the ante-diluvial atmosphere of parts of the UK is more congenial for managerial dinosaurs than the innovation-orientated USA.

The philosophy of the nature of management, of what a manager is, and of what he should do has been a subject provoking long hours of discussion in business-school common-rooms throughout the world. Paradoxically, it has been of less concern in those business offices where management was actually taking place and managing. One might in fact guess that the subject of good management had been completely ignored by good managers. They automatically know what it is: they are it, whether defined or not! This naturally leads one to question whether the business schools are wasting valuable hours in unprofitable sophistry; because if the topic is insufficient to prompt the manager's attention, is it important enough to warrant the academic's thoughts? Are the academics guilty of using a microscope to build the molehill into the mountain? Should one follow the attitude of the man on the job, the manager who argues, 'Enough of this nonsense. I know what I am and what my job entails. Now let's get on with it without any more of this philosophical balderdash.'

The truth undoubtedly lies between the two extremes. It must be clear that in spite of these criticisms good management does owe a debt to academic thinking; for the nature of the difference between good and the bad in management is becoming better understood very much as a direct result of the academic's promptings and explorations. One thus cannot really be antagonistic to academic efforts: one must try to break down the barriers to the much fuller industrial role which academic thinkers ought to play. Management clearly needs help, research and advice to improve the quality of its management decision-making. In this it can well use academic intelligence and impartiality. But first management must be given some sign that the academic word may be trusted; that the would-be advisers have a feeling for real problems and are not completely divorced from industrial activity. The criticism of narrow and backward academic thinking may not therefore quite extend to the extreme of advocating 'Peoples Universities' or New Polytechnics as a realistic panacea to present dissatisfactions. Such creations might bring into being new and up-to-date industrial-academic partnerships: but they would not (and could not) alter the outlook and climate of the older universities who nonetheless may have a valuable industrial contribution to make. This can only be achieved by their self-realization of the need for urgency, identity, involvement and keeping in touch with the industrial world.

Perhaps also one should even be surprised that academic researchers have so far been able to achieve so much in spite of the enormous handicaps which they have placed upon themselves. For their achievements really have been considerable in advancing management's awareness of business techniques.

At the level of the obvious any follower of the management literature of the past decade will be encouraged by the progress towards a better management – the buzzwords roll off the tongue from work study, O. and M., investment appraisal, management information systems, manpower budgeting, long-range planning, PPBS and Cost-Effectiveness. It will be noted that the ideas have moved from the detailed to the general, from work-study to corporate and long-term objectives. This seems to be a key feature of the modern view of management, the new logic which (very sensibly) begins by argument about what is the objective, both short- and long-term. And this holds good whether the organization is a company, a local government community or a central government. Too often in the past we have overlooked the need to begin our planning exercises by defining objectives, have assumed that objectives were known, agreed and understood, and in our gleeful suboptimizing of detailed areas of organizational activity, we felt that we were making the right contribution to the overall effort. And in the absence of organizational objectives, who was there gently to correct us of the fallacies? One can only take heart that objectives are now being argued out so thoroughly. They must prevent a lot of useless mole work.

It may seem incomprehensible that some firms exist without any more objective than being there. The daily round undermines the company objective and management continues to 'guide' the organization 'successfully' only so long as conditions remain static. In a dynamic situation, the forces of rapid change immediately produce problems of labour, capital, plant, equipment or commodities which are beyond the capacity of such complacent management to overcome. They have so little vision of forward planning that they barely recognize the nature of today, nor even begin to envisage what the shape of tomorrow (and the day after!) will be.

This is why the comparison which William Morris raises between management and science is so apt: the similarity is essentially one of thought-processes and reasoning, and not one of techniques of operation. By emphasizing logical analysis of the business situation as the key feature of good management, one stems the rush to the therapeutic ragbag of operational techniques. One always suspects that doctors should look beyond mere symptoms before making their diagnoses; and this is no less true for managers. They need to be able to abstract the key features of their system, to perceive the logical pattern which underlies the immediate situation, and to act for tomorrow as well as today.

If businesses are able to have clearly-stated and agreed objectives, the answers to their problems become so much closer, for definition of objectives almost invariably leads to recognition of methods and measures of attainment. The methods in themselves usually provide alternative procedures for approaching the solution and there is an optimum strategy identifiable by the criteria of 'least cost' or 'most profit'. This is the cost-effectiveness approach and the emphasis on objectives in this book is established by William Morris and followed up by George Taylor, while the practicalities of measurement are taken up by Hal Bierman and Ray Cuninghame-Green. The latter writers also logically extend their approach to identifying the best alternative from the ones open to choice.

Management Decision-Making thus covers the salient features of the Cost-Effectiveness philosophy of management and tries to see what the manager's problems really are; rather than following the Operations Research approach which one might drily describe as trying to see what problems the researchers would like to tackle, where the interest in the intricacy of the research *per se* is allowed to overcloud and often exclude the relevance to practical managerial needs. If we could make one big change to modern management it would be to give managers the ability to see what their company objectives are and what they really ought to be. Too often enterprises lose momentum not only by not knowing what they *ought* to be trying to do but even by not knowing what they *are* trying to do.

This is a major contribution that logically-ordered science can help to make to management decision-making. It can be used to discover objectives and by doing so it will imply a means of attainment, a menu for choice and a measure of success. Although decision-making is only one part of management activity, the planning processes – together with human relations – form the most important elements. In these planning processes, management science is not a service to managers but becomes an integral part of the management function. It is thereby made indispensable to objective setting, and good management decision-making.

Finally, it is suggested that many readers will find it helpful to omit chapters 9, 17 and 21 on their first reading of this book. Each of these chapters contains technical detail for the sections by Hal Bierman, Ray Cuninghame-Green and David Couts which is not imperative for appreciation of the rest of the argument. The chapters may be covered at a second reading where the reader wishes to go into depth on the calculational procedures.

A guide to further reading

STAFFORD BEER, *Management Science; The business use of Operational Research* (Aldus, 1967)

Full of wisdom about the very nature and existence of management as a logical pattern of activity.

JOHN ARGENTI, *Corporate Planning; a practical guide* (Allen and Unwin, 1968)
A first-class introduction to the new approach to objective setting and operational planning for company activity.

BILLY E. GOETZ, *Quantitative Methods: a survey and guide for managers* (McGraw-Hill, 1965)
Covers the full range of quantitative techniques in a straightforward way and attempts to relate the methods to the underlying managerial principles and philosophies.

ROBERT SCHLAIFER, *Probability and Statistics for Business Decisions* (McGraw-Hill, 1959)
A basic text which is the foundation of much quantitative reasoning in business and management. Not easy, but very worthwhile the effort to understand.

SELECTED REFERENCES

Enquiry into the flow of candidates in science and technology into higher education (The Dainton Report, HMSO, 1968)

The flow into employment of scientists, engineers and technologists (The Swann Report, HMSO, 1968)

The employment of highly specialized graduates: a comparative study in the UK and the USA (HMSO, 1968)

Ernest Rudd and Stephen Hatch, *Graduate study and after* (Weidenfeld and Nicolson, 1968)

R. G. Brown, 'The corporate integration of operational research'. (Edinburgh Conference of the Operational Research Society, 1968)

Part I

MANAGEMENT DECISIONS – ART OR SCIENCE?

WILLIAM T. MORRIS

Professor of Industrial Engineering
The Ohio State University

William T. Morris is a graduate of the Massachusetts Institute of Technology. He obtained his M Sc and Ph D at the Ohio State University, where he has been associated in teaching, writing research and consultancy since 1953.

He is an acknowledged expert on management decision-making, combining the first-class qualities of a teacher with those of a writer. His teaching honours include the Ohio State University Alumni Award for Distinguished Teaching (1965), and the Charles E. MacQuigg Award for Teaching Excellence (1967). The quality of his written contribution to management thinking was recognized in 1963 when the Academy of Management and the McKinsey Foundation chose his book *Management Science in Action* as one of the five outstanding books of the year.

His articles frequently appear in the leading journals of management and they are eagerly read by students, teachers and experienced managers throughout the world. His full-length books include:

Engineering Economy – The Analysis of Management Decisions (Richard D. Irwin, Inc., 1960; rev. ed. 1964).

Analysis for Materials Handling Management (Richard D. Irwin, Inc., 1962).

Management Science in Action (Richard D. Irwin, Inc., 1963).

The Analysis of Management Decisions (Richard D. Irwin, Inc., 1964).

The Capacity Decision System (Richard D. Irwin, Inc., 1967).

Decentralization in Management Systems (The Ohio State University Press, 1967).

Management Science – a Bayesian Integration (Prentice-Hall, Inc., 1968).

Chapter One

FRAMING THE QUESTION

HISTORICAL VERSIONS OF THE QUESTION

VIGOROUS discussion of the proper or possible relation between management and science goes back to the late nineteenth century. As is so often the case, these discussions do not seem to have produced widely satisfying answers, but they have shown us the overwhelming importance of searching for the right questions. Insights into the ways in which art, science, and management can be understood together have come from successive reformulations of hypotheses, leading over the years to the ways in which we presently consider the problem. Even though we must greatly oversimplify the process, it is worthwhile to examine enough of this history to avoid repeating its major inquiries ourselves.

When we now speak of 'management science' we seem to hope by this ordering of the words to distinguish our questions from those that arose out of the 'scientific management' movement around the turn of the century. In using the latter label for their ideas, F. W. Taylor and his disciples in the Taylor Society provided, quite unintentionally, an inflammatory basis for many years of debate. (1) Taylor was the sort of man who was neither bound by conventional patterns of thought, nor lacking in the courage to put his unconventional conclusions into practice. He made a major contribution in bringing to the problem of job design the notions of precise measurement and experimental methods for finding better ways of working. He insisted that the planning of work in the factory is of such importance that it should be institutionalized in a scheme of functional foremanship. Taylor's difficulties and those of his followers arose not so much out of this sort of innovation, as out of two directions in which others over-generalized his ideas.

The first difficulty followed from the presumption that job design could be made a matter of science in the image of classical physics. Precise measurement and experimental methods were important, but to be a science one must produce simple, general laws of wide applicability. It was this attempt to find a Newtonian system for the phenomena of work which led to much dispute. We are still discovering that the nature of work must be understood in terms of a constellation of physical, physiological, psychological as well as social and economic factors. Those who claimed to have found 'the one best way' of doing a job simply invited attempts at contradiction.

The other sort of overgeneralization which distorted Taylor's intentions arose out of the exciting possibility of applying the aspects of science which Taylor had brought to the problems of the shop foreman at higher levels in the management structure. Taylor himself seemed to appreciate at least some of the difficulties that this effort would encounter, but there were others who seemed all too ready to leap ahead. Soon there was discussion of what might be expected when all levels of management had been made scientific and this discussion was shortly followed by asser-tions that management was a science or at least an emergent science. Such statements immediately provoked a full measure of heated response. Management, it was claimed, was an art in which proficiency depended on the accumula-tion of years of experience and the ability to make subtle, unverbalized judgements. Such an art could clearly never be 'reduced' to a science.

References to 'science' in these debates seem to have been references to physics, in some ways the most successful of the sciences. Questions as to whether management was a science or whether it would become one, could often be understood as questions about similarities between management and physics. On the surface of it, the two activities are quite dissimilar. Physics is thought of as being characterized by general laws of wide applicability producing highly reliable predictions, by carefully controlled laboratory experiments yielding very precise measurements, and by a pervading atmosphere of objectivity and impersonality. In short, we often think of classical physics as having pretty thoroughly eliminated uncertainty about those phenomena which it has investigated.

Management, on the other hand, is often thought of as an activity in which experiments are difficult to control, most interesting aspects cannot be measured precisely, general laws are completely lacking, each management problem is viewed as unique, and the intuitive or 'judgemental' application of subjective experience reigns supreme. Indeed, management is an activity pervaded by high uncertainty and apparently in no interesting way like physics. This difficulty has arisen whenever some management phenomenon has been measured with precision, perhaps with a stop watch, and some attempt has been made at expressing the phenomenon in mathematical terms. Then management began in some small way to look like physics, and people were tempted to suppose that in some grand way, management could be like physics. Managers themselves have been justifiably impatient with any such proposal since it was so obviously out of touch with what they took to be the real nature of their work. In their impatience, however, they often succumbed to the temptation of asserting that science could in no useful way be related to management and management must forever remain an art in which experience counts for nearly everything.

As time passed psychologists, sociologists and economists began to take an interest in problems of direct concern to managers. It became clear that these sciences had something to contribute to problems, for example, of motivation, leadership style, or pricing policy. This had two interesting effects, the first of which was simply to associate management problems with the social and behavioral sciences, emphasizing the ways in which they differed from the layman's view of classical physics. The precision of measurement and prediction, the simple general laws, and the ease of manipulative experimentation which formed the image of physics, began to recede as necessary conditions for a science.

The second effect of association with the behavioral sciences was to suggest that training in these fields might be an appropriate preparation for management. With such an academic foundation, some felt that management could now be called a profession. This seemed to mean, on the model of medicine, that management was an art which was supported and illuminated by science. As in the case of medicine, this left open the troublesome question of how much was art and how much science, and there were those who wished to call scientific any activity to which science made some small contribution.

Somewhat aside from all this, there began a development in the 1920s which was to be a most important intellectual precedent. Walter Shewhart undertook to apply the methods of statistics to problems of quality control in production and procurement.* This was interesting because it involved an early attempt to go beyond simply providing the manager with information and to formulate more or less explicitly the manager's decision problem. By using probability theory as a language for expressing the uncertainty which is such a prominent feature of interesting management decision problems, Shewhart broke out of the deterministic idiom of early physics. Indeed, the main thrust of Operations Research after World War II may be interpreted as a further clarification of the possibilities for using science to deal with the uncertainty that plagues manage-

---

* The pioneering work of William Sealy Gosset is almost invariably overlooked in this context. Gosset (1876–1937) was one of the first industrial scientists to use statistics for sampling, testing, control and reliability of product in his work both at St James' Brewery and at Park Royal when he joined Arthur Guinness and Son Ltd from Oxford in 1899. He is much more familiar for his writings as 'Student' and for his 't-distribution'.

ment. One should not look to science to reduce management to matters of certainty, but rather to express and suggest responses to the inevitable uncertainty of managerial decisions. The notion of a 'calculated risk' could become a matter of actual calculation rather than a simple way of saying one had been unlucky.*

Along with Operations Research came the digital computer and still further reformulations of the problem of art and science in management. There has been talk of using the computer to replace middle managers. Computers have been credited with designing a new product, managing an investment portfolio, discovering an optimal inventory policy, and so on. Here again, one response has been that the judgements of an experienced manager can never be made by a computer. Computer technology has simply raised older versions of our questions in a new jargon.

Out of all this one may draw two important suggestions. In the first place, it is not very useful to ask whether management is or is not a science. The useful question seems to be, 'to what extent can science be used to illuminate the dark and difficult corners of the art of management?' Secondly, what we must look for are good divisions of labor between the experienced manager on the one hand and the analyst supported by his digital computer on the other. Roughly speaking, we would like to give to the manager those tasks which he can do best and to 'science' those tasks which it can do best.†

MODERN VERSIONS OF THE QUESTION

From our present vantage point, something like the following appear to be useful ways of asking about art and science management.

* The calculation of this risk is explored by Hal Bierman in Part II and by Ray Cunninghame-Green in Part IV.

† See, for example, the development of this theme with regard to forecasting in M. J. Slonim, *Guide to Sampling* (ed. G. A. Yewdall; Pan, 1968; pp. 81–82) and the applications given by David Couts in Part V.

1. What is the optimum division of labor between the unaided intuitive or judgemental procedures of the manager, and the analytical and explicit methods of the management scientist? To what extent should the manager delegate parts of his decision process?

2. If we view both science and management as essentially learning processes, are the efficient methods of learning in science also the efficient methods of learning in management? Can the methods of science become to some extent the methods of management?

3. If one agrees for a moment, that a management decision will often have intuitive or judgemental inputs from the manager as well as explicit and analytical inputs from the management scientist, how are these two types of input to be weighted and combined? Can we only say that it is a combination of art and science, or can we say something about how they are to be integrated?

Before setting out to explore these questions, it is worth noting that they picture the manager largely as a decision maker. One should not suppose that all a manager does is make decisions, nor possibly is this even his most important activity. Typically he spends the largest portion of his time communicating, instructing, influencing, justifying, checking, and so on. In terms of the manager's 'daily round', our attention is drawn to a limited part of management. To explore these questions then, we will begin with a look at the psychology of the management decision process to see a little more clearly what we might mean by 'art'.

Chapter Two

ART AS INTUITION

IF we set out simply to ask a manager to tell us how he goes about making an important decision, we may very well encounter the traditional difficulties of introspective psychology. Typically the manager finds it difficult if not impossible to verbalize what he does. He may be unwilling even to attempt to verbalize or he may put us off with oversimplified, *ad hoc* explanations of how a decision was made. In this situation he is not alone, for experienced professionals in science, mathematics, medicine, and many other fields find that as they become more and more effective, their work has a growing intuitive or unverbalized content. It is common to speak of this as the 'artistic' part of these professions and for our purposes it suffices to take 'intuitive' as a synonym for 'artistic'. Although the manager may not be willing or able to explain how, he is able to make decisions, often acting quickly in the face of what appear to be a complex situation. He proceeds to a decision not by conscious, step-by-step, logical reasoning, but by a kind of intuitive leap. Experience has told him that he may rely on the results of this implicit, partially sub-conscious process which he may wish to call mature managerial judgement.

The intuitive manager finds it difficult to report what aspects of the situation his perceptual processes have selected, or how he has conceptualized the decision. He does not explicitly draw upon his memory, nor can he indicate clearly the inferential process that takes him from these inputs to a conclusion. But, of course, the brilliant scientist or mathematician exhibits much the same sort of behavior. The interesting difference is that in science and mathematics one does not simply accept the results, but rather tests them by analysis and experiment. The manager, however, has traditionally tested the results of his intuition in the laboratory of actual experience. The fact that these tests have sometimes been costly is really the basic motivation for management science.

The intuitive manager is willing to act on the untested products of his decision process because intuition has several very appealing properties. Typically his intuition has been trustworthy. He has developed it over a considerable period of time, learning from some of his mistakes and explaining away others, so that in retrospect he feels that intuition has generally served him well. It has become habitual for him to approach decisions in this way since he has had little else on which to rely. He has come to regard intuition as a primary asset and will be suspicious of all attempts to tamper with it. He finds intuition a gratifying process which seems to utilize his unique sensitivity to the decision problem. It is a private, mysterious skill developed through long experience. Finally, he may find intuition very well adapted to the context of his affairs. It permits quick decisions in the face of both ambiguity and uncertainty. It can be made to meet the constraints of time, cost, and knowledge imposed by the environment in which he works.

It is hardly surprising if a manager thus finds the sort of explicit, deliberate, logical methods advocated by the management scientist somewhat less than welcome. For the manager these suggestions may well appear to be untrustworthy, ill-adapted to the context of affairs, and perhaps most importantly, quite unnecessary. It is impossible at this stage of our knowledge to produce very much evidence as to the general effectiveness of managerial intuition. In a sense, every time management science succeeds in making a contribution to a decision problem, one has a specific demonstration that intuitive methods in management can sometimes be improved upon. Over against these instances, however, are others in which intuition appears to reign supreme and analysis is so far unable to make any improve-

ments. There is some evidence that complex financial
decisions can be understood with relatively simple analytical
means,* and some have suggested that many of the management decisions which now appear highly judgemental will
yield to reproduction by the management scientist. From
clinical psychology there is evidence that even the seemingly
highly refined intuitive decisions made by the clinician
might be effectively replaced by statistical procedures. These
are, however, matters which will require much more study
to produce anything like wide agreement. It is perhaps,
most useful to view the program of management science as
part of such an undertaking.

Under present conditions the explicit analytical and
experimental work of the management scientist cannot be
regarded as simply attempts to replace the manager's
intuition. Rather one must think of management science as
having four objectives:

1. To check the results of a manager's intuition just as a
   scientist checks his hypotheses by explicit, communi-
   cable methods. It may be that the main difference
   between managers and scientists lies in their relative
   willingness or unwillingness to rely on unaided
   intuitions. The contribution of management science is
   to test before implementation, rather than relying on
   the costly knowledge gained from actual experience.
2. To extend and supplement the manager's intuition
   in those cases in which it breaks down and fails to lead
   him to a conclusion. Situations which are novel, highly
   complex, and which appear to the manager to be
   unusually ambiguous and uncertain may produce such
   breakdowns in his standard methods of choice.
3. To help the manager to develop intuition by improving
   the effectiveness with which he learns from experience.
4. To discover those decision situations in which his
   intuitive results can be reproduced and perhaps

* The point is explored by George Taylor in Part III.

improved by explicit methods, thus permitting these to be delegated. The aim of such delegation is to free the manager to attend to other decisions which appear to yield only to his special skills.

The methodical progression toward such objectives seems to require in the first instance some understanding of the ways in which intuition may not serve the manager well. Our next step is thus to propose a model of the decision process, the function of which is to suggest some hypotheses about the inadequacies of intuition. Hopefully, the tentative identification of these weaknesses will suggest specific ways in which management science might contribute.

It may be wise, however, to pause for a word of caution. There is the possibility that by working with an effective intuitive manager, by encouraging him to be explicit and self-conscious, and by seeming to make his problems more and more complex, we may actually injure his intuitive skill. There appears as yet to be little evidence that such a thing does happen, but the possibility is in the minds of some investigators in the field. If we are to maintain some objectivity about the possibilities for science in management, it would seem important to treat the well-developed intuition with care and explore it with caution.

We love life

You enjoy life now, and you'll still want to do so when you retire. But you'll need money for this.

£10,000 when you retire
by taking out now a Prudential Endowment
Assurance. For more details, complete
and return this card.

Some examples
The value of Prudential policies has been
amply demonstrated over the years, as
is shown by these examples of payments on
claims under Ordinary Branch with-profits
endowment assurances for £5,000 taken
out in the U.K., and which matured at age
65 on 1st April, 1972.

Age at entry	30	40	50
Sum assured	£5,000	£5,000	£5,000
Bonuses*	6,845	5,530	3,525
	£11,845	£10,530	£8,525

Bonuses on future maturities cannot be guaranteed

PNB/5/72/1164/FP(2075)

BUSINESS REPLY SERVICE

LICENCE No. K.E. 1511

The Chief General Manager
THE PRUDENTIAL ASSURANCE CO. LTD.

142 HOLBORN BARS
LONDON EC1N 2NH

We love life

You enjoy life now, and you'll still want to do so when you retire. But you'll need money for this.

£10,000 when you retire
by taking out now a Prudential Endowment Assurance. For more details, complete and return this card.

Some examples
The value of Prudential policies has been amply demonstrated over the years, as is shown by these examples of payments on claims under Ordinary Branch with-profits endowment assurances for £5,000 taken out in the U.K., and which matured at age 65 on 1st April, 1972.

Age at entry	30	40	50
Sum assured	£5,000	£5,000	£5,000
Bonuses*	6,845	5,530	3,525
	£11,845	£10,530	£8,525

*Bonuses on future maturities cannot be guaranteed

Chapter Three

A MODEL OF THE MANAGEMENT-DECISION PROCESS

In outlining a model of the decision process, we do not, of course, presume to suggest that we are indicating the way any manager thinks, nor are we suggesting anything particular about the division of labor between a manager's conscious and his subconscious mental processes. We are simply adopting the fairly standard psychological tactic of using a model which has as its purpose the raising of interesting hypotheses which could be tested. It is useful to think of a manager 'behaving as if' he used the process we will describe because this sensitizes us to effects that should be watched for in his behavior.

We might suppose that the decision process begins with the perception of some sort of stimulus which suggests to the manager that a decision situation is at hand. A machine has broken down, a competitor has just launched a new product, or last week's production report has just been received. This initial perception is supplemented from the contents of the manager's memory to form an initial conceptualization of the situation. Indeed what we mean by a decision is really a conceptualization of a decision situation. There is, we suppose, a rather complex set of interactions among the processes of perception, recall, and conceptualization. We do not perceive everything that is around us and available to our senses, nor do we recall everything that has been a part of our past experience. Perception and recall are thus selective processes and by selecting, they present the decision-maker with an abstracted or simplified conceptualization. The key to understanding any decision may thus lie in discovering how this simplification takes place.

What one perceives is controlled in part by his past experience and thus by what he recalls. What he recalls is in part controlled by the stimuli which he receives. One tends further to perceive things which one can fit into some sort of conceptual structure or which one can 'make some sense' out of. One of the things which characterizes the trained or experienced observer is the presence of conceptual structures which control or sensitize his perceptions. He is prepared to notice 'important' or 'significant' things which others may miss. In similar fashion, what one 'learns' and thus readily recalls are those things which one is able to fit into patterns or conceptually organize. Generally, we suppose that conceptual models are necessary to 'make sense' of the vast perceptual complexity and confusion which the environment presents.

The manager's initial conceptualization of the choice problem may be characterized by clarity and low uncertainty, particularly if the problem is a routine or familiar one. In such cases the manager's response may be an immediate willingness to decide and to act. At this point it may be clear that the general form of our model is a familiar one in psychology for it raises hypotheses about the dynamics of stimulus, conception, and response.

Alternatively, the initial conceptualization may be characterized by confusion, doubts, missing information; in short, it may be characterized by high uncertainty. The manager may thus be dissatisfied with his conceptualization and unwilling to rely upon it as a basis for decision and action. Then, we suppose, he undertakes some program for the reduction of his uncertainty. Being uncertain that he is considering all of the reasonably available courses of action, he may undertake a program of search for additional alternatives. If he does so and additional actions are discovered, these become a part of his modified conceptualization of the decision problem. The crucial question here is how long to go on searching for additional actions before initiating some other response to the decision situation. Of course, after responding in some other way, he may later return to search again.

For any course of action under consideration, uncertainty as to its consequences may prompt the gathering of additional data in order to yield better predictions of the results. Here again, the crucial question is how much additional data to gather before responding in some other way. This of course, is the analog of the scientist's problem as to how many times he should replicate his experiment. The manager may alternate between searching for additional actions and gathering data on those discovered, terminating any search-prediction process when he has discovered an action which is in some sense 'satisfactory' to him.

A third response to his conceptualization may be what we will call value clarification. While we sometimes tend to assume that a manager's objectives or goals are perfectly clear and operationally defined, this is, it would appear, seldom the case. A basic reason for being unwilling to proceed with a decision may be a need to become clearer as to what one's objectives are, and how the predicted consequences of an action are related to these objectives. The traditional business decision involves a choice between high profit–high risk alternatives and low profit–low risk alternatives. For many decision-makers, it is a matter of considerable difficulty to decide just how much possibility for profit they are willing to relinquish in return for additional certainty of obtaining a profit. Every new investor in stocks has experienced the difficulty of being explicit to his broker about the tradeoff between profit and risk consistent with his investment objectives. Similarly, the firm which considers installing a digital computer may find difficulty in balancing the potential monetary saving against the undesirable consequences of laying off a portion of its office staff. Again the crucial question is how much effort to devote to value clarification before going on to other responses to the decision situation.

We suppose that these responses, to whatever extent and in

whatever sequence they are pursued, result ultimately in a modified conceptualization of the decision problem which the manager is willing to use as a basis for choice. The sorts of responses involved may easily be thought of as learning activities. Note also that they may be undertaken typically without committing oneself to a decision. One should not suppose that the manager reaches the point of being certain that he has considered all of the possible courses of action, being certain as to their consequences, or being certain as to what his objectives are or how they will be served by the actions in question. Much as he would like to be certain, the pressure of ongoing affairs, the cost both in time and money of the responses involved, and the reasonable willingness to tolerate some uncertainty, lead him to something short of an indefinite postponement of the decision. Once again the crucial question is of the degree of uncertainty he is willing to tolerate and the degree of uncertainty it would be 'reasonable' for him to tolerate. When is it rational for him to stipulate that his current conceptualization of the decision is adequate and that he is willing to act 'as if' his current conceptualization represented reality?

When he has reached the point of achieving a satisfactory basis for decision, presumably he decides and ultimately his decision is implemented. The results of implementation are, in a more or less explicit manner, introduced into his own experience and into the firm's data bank, where they form a potential basis for subsequent decisions. When this assimilation of results is routinized we often call it a management control system. Of course it is basically just another sort of learning or adaptive system.

Chapter Four

ANALYSING THE DECISION PROCESS

SELECTIVITY AND SIMPLIFICATION

As we reflect on this model of the manager's decision process, it is not difficult to formulate hypotheses about the ways in which simplifications and distortions may creep in and about the ways in which management science might supplement and illuminate the art. We might begin by considering the ways in which the decision-maker might achieve perceptual and conceptual simplifications of a complex problem. All of us must do this because of the cognitive limitations of our unaided minds. We must simplify problems in order to make them intellectually tractable. The capacity of the mind limits the number of alternatives, the list of constraints, the amount of past experience, and so on, which can be consciously dealt with by the unaided mind. The key to understanding choice behavior is to understand the pattern which is used in reducing the endless complexity of the actual situation to a manageable conception of the choice problem.

We may usefully raise some hypotheses about the ways in which this simplification takes place. For example:

1. Resort to 'rules of thumb'. The notions that we 'ought to keep 30 days' inventory on hand', or that one 'should expect an investment to pay out in three years' are examples of conventional simplifications which often serve in place of detailed analyses.

2. Appeal to a System of Categories. Often policy categories are used to place decisions in broad classes. Each class is characterized by a particular response

which has been previously determined to be more or less appropriate for the members of the class. Generally speaking, the broader and more inclusive the policy categories, the less effective is likely to be the categorical response to any particular decision.

3. Suppress Uncertainty. Clearly one of the more prominent modes of simplification is to regard events and quantities about which many people would agree there is considerable uncertainty, as known with certainty. One may ignore unlikely events, consider only a single possible set of future conditions, consider average values, or some such device to avoid the complexity of dealing with uncertainty. The conservative person deals only with the worst events that may happen, the optimist with the best, some with only the most probable events, and so on.

4. Adopt a Near Planning Horizon. A decision often has consequences which extend far into the future which a full analysis of the problem would examine. Typically, the further in the future an event, the greater one's uncertainty about it and the further in the future an income, the less one is willing to pay for it in the present. Much thinking about decisions is probably characterized by simplification through the use of a relatively near planning horizon in which events are considered for a short period in the future but not beyond that point. Similarly one might simplify by limiting the consideration of past experience to only the rather recent past.

5. Spurious Resolution of Value Conflicts. Attempts to consider several objectives, the attainment of some of which almost always requires the retreat from others, is a serious source of complexity. The need to resolve these goal or value conflicts may lead to suppressing some of them. Simplification may be sought by restricting consideration of the values of consequences to those dimensions which are most easily measurable or most 'tangible'. Thus one may consider profit, units of

production, and so on, while suppressing the complexity of human attitudes, and social or moral values.

NEED-DETERMINED DISTORTIONS

Wishful thinking is our common phrase for the sort of distortion that creeps into perceiving and conceptualizing as a result of basic needs and desires. Psychologists have been much interested in this need-determined sort of distortion because we ourselves are often unaware of it. We consider three hypotheses about the effects of needs in the decision process.

1. Habitual ways of viewing a decision situation arise because a conception which meets the needs of one situation is uncritically applied to others. Habits might be thought of as ways of economizing the limited capacity of the mind. Rather than develop a conception which tries to account objectively for each individual choice situation, one simply resorts by analogy to customary conceptions or tends to fit decisions into categories previously developed. Organizations develop such habits and they tend to get formalized into policies or routines for decision-making. These habitual conceptions are perpetuated because they satisfy one's need to respond to the pressure of affairs which overtax the conceptualizing capacity of the mind. Habits also help to satisfy the need for being able to defend a decision in an organization. Certainly a widely-used defence for an unsuccessful decision is the claim that it was based on 'the way we always do it', or that it was placed in a category for which a policy was already determined. The problem of extinguishing habits which satisfy these sorts of needs is often referred to as the problem of overcoming resistance to change. The particular mark of a habitual conception which has begun to lose its objective relation to the choice situation is to answer the question, 'Why did you choose this way?' with the explanation, 'Well, I guess because we always do it this way'.

2. One's conceptions of choice situations tend to move

toward a view of the situation as the person would like to see it, and not necessarily as it is. Expectations are not independent of desires and conceptions play a part in satisfying needs when actions prove inadequate to the task. If a person finds himself in very limited control of a situation, to some extent quite powerless to act in a satisfying way, then at least he can remake his conceptualization of the situation so as to view it more satisfactorily. If the need for certainty and confidence in decision-making cannot be achieved through predictive knowledge and the ability to control events, then perhaps conceptions will become subjectively free of doubt and uncertainty in response to this need.

Perception is a selective process which tends to give structure to the vastly complicated situations encountered in experience. In perceiving a situation, some elements of it 'stand out' more clearly than others. The psychological term is 'figure and ground', the figure being those elements perceived most clearly against the suppressed background of the remainder. The psychologist goes on to hypothesize that the elements which tend to stand out as figure are at least in part controlled by needs, in the sense of having previously been perceived in satisfying situations. This, of course, works as the result of fears as well as desires. This kind of hypothesis seems to have great possibilities for sensitizing one to the kind of subjective images managers might be expected to work with. At the most obvious level one would expect the part of the environment which stands out in a manager's perception to depend upon such things as whether or not he had been making decisions during the Great Depression, the labor strife of the thirties, the Second World War, the postwar booms and recessions, and so on.

3. Finally, conceptions of choice situations get distorted because of the social and organizational processes which lead a person to view things in ways accepted by his associates. Socially shared views, which come not so much from contact with reality as from the need to agree to belong, or to avoid questioning the views of a group, are part of most decisions.

An individual decision-maker, a part of an organization, experiences a demand from his superiors that his behavior be reliable, predictable, and in a general sense within control. They need to know how he is going to make decisions so they can account for, and plan on, the basis of his behavior. He thus finds it increasingly necessary to conform to the organization's way of conceptualizing decision situations or to follow the organizational rules. The rules and conventions tend to become important, no longer because of their original objective effectiveness for achieving organizational goals but rather for their own sake. It becomes less important to make a decision so as to advance the objectives of the organization and more important to make a decision acceptable in the organizational process. This leads to viewing decisions as falling into one or another of a relatively small number of organizationally sanctioned categories. Thus, conceptualization of choice situations becomes a rigid process. This may well mean that the decisions are less and less successful at the same time as they are becoming more reliable, predictable, and defensible within the organization.

LEARNING

Of special interest to us will be the sorts of cognitive distortion that one might expect to discover in the learning process. This is the process of assimilating new information into established conceptions. The basic problem is how much weight to give to past experience and how much to new data and information which may become available. Overconfidence and strong predispositions suggest one may be giving too much weight to past experience. Decision-makers may be distracted by irrelevant events or attach too much importance to critical incidents. There is the suspicion that when people have the opportunity deliberately to buy information which is relevant to a decision they tend to pay more for information that is consistent with their own opinions and objectives, and generally fail to wring all the uncertainty reduction from the data that is logically possible.

Chapter Five

THE USES OF SCIENCE

AT this stage of our analysis of the manager's decision process, it is hardly surprising to suggest that the role of management science is to support and extend this decision process at its weaker points. We will, however, offer some more explicit hypotheses about the ways in which this division of labor between the intuitive manager and management science might be worked out. First, it should be clear to the manager that there are some things which cannot reasonably be accomplished. Management science cannot guarantee him a good outcome or that he will make the 'right decision'. It can only help him to work toward decisions which are reasoned and appear sensible in the light of the knowledge it is reasonable to have in hand prior to acting. A good decision can be made with deliberation and care, but a good outcome depends upon chance. A man who must get from New York to Los Angeles, and for whom time is more important than money, may well decide to fly. If his plane crashes en route and he is injured, the outcome was not good, but this does not make the decision less reasonable. Indeed, one test is whether or not he remains satisfied with the decision, no matter what the outcome. The best we can hope for are decisions which will appear to be satisfactory to the decision-maker, even from a hindsight viewpoint.

One cannot, of course, relieve a manager of the necessity of sacrificing some of his objectives in return for the achievement of others. It is seldom that courses of action are found which simultaneously move one toward all of his goals. Nor can one relieve him of all uncertainty. Science may be able to help him express his uncertainty, to modify it reasonably in the face of new information, and to act with deliberation in spite of it, but it cannot make the process of deciding an easy one for him. In fact, it may well become more difficult. What is proposed by science will require considerable effort and is clearly not the sort of thing that will be used in every instance of management decision-making. The task is to show what benefits might be expected if one does invest the effort to be explicit and logical in deciding. Only by suggesting the possible payoffs, can one give the decision-maker a basis for deciding which of his problems are important and uncertain enough to warrant the required investment of effort.

On the positive side, let us examine some hypotheses as to what management science might contribute to the problem of establishing the goals of the organization, the problem of predicting the consequences of various policies, and the problem of learning from experience. Setting goals or objectives for an organization has traditionally been *the* management prerogative, and it should be clear that management science proposes no challenge to this tradition. Goals have, however, been largely matters of implicit understanding and agreement among the top managers, and few attempts have been made to explicitly transmit these objectives throughout the organization. Goals were spoken of in broad and general terms but there was seldom any clear statement of just what combinations of risk and profit expectation were or were not acceptable to the firm, for example. The objectives are not transmitted to new managers by explicit statement, but rather by an extended process of assimilating 'the way things are done in this company'. Management science has thus found it difficult to go beyond studies in which expected cost or expected profit were treated as the explicit goals. The final reports of such studies must go to top management who somehow integrate them with their implicit views of the firm's objectives.

There are now beginning to be some interesting reasons for altering this situation and suggesting to the manager that goals be made more explicit. What is sought are not more elaborate general pronouncements about the firm's value system, but rather specific statements which are sufficiently operational to permit decisive application to actual decision situations. That is, management science would like to get at the organization's indifference maps or utility functions. (2)

There are three purposes which may be served if managers are willing to make their goals explicit in this way. First, is the increased possibility for the delegation of decisions. As long as the firm's value system is implicit, top managers must make the value system operative by giving personal attention to decisions. Not even ordinary inventory control decisions can be delegated without some explicit rendering of values. Here, indeed, is where the current movement toward greater delegation appears to be stalled. Secondly, as we have earlier suggested, the decision process may be blocked because the manager is simply not clear about his value system. When offered an opportunity to install a machine accounting system which will require the dismissal of x persons and promises a net savings of y per year, he may not be at all clear that 'y justifies x'. One of the less developed possibilities of management science is that of helping him become clear by offering a conceptual structure within which to make his values explicit, to see their inter-relationships, and to formulate in his own mind the tradeoffs which he feels are appropriate for the firm. Explicitness is simply offered as a possible means for assisting in the resolution of value conflicts.

Perhaps the most difficult aspect of goal setting is that of coming to grips with the multiple, conflicting nature of most value structures. In deciding which of two houses to buy, we compare them on the basis of price, number of rooms, tax rate, style, location, and so on. It is relatively easy to compare the houses one attribute at a time, but the difficulty arises when these comparisons must be somehow aggregated into an overall preference. Similar problems occur when one must choose between development projects, plant locations, candidates for vice-president, and, in fact, in nearly all interesting decisions. Here the early results of some experiments in the division of labor have been especially suggestive. (3) It has been proposed that the multiple goal problem be approached by having the manager compare his opportunities on the basis of one attribute at a time, evaluating the houses first on the basis of price, second on the basis of number of rooms and so on. These simple comparisons, judgements, or ratings are rather easy for one to make. It is then proposed that these be combined, not by the manager, but by the analyst and his computer into an overall evaluation. The surprising result is that even if the logic which is used to aggregate the basic preference statements is rather simple and straightforward, the results seem to meet with two responses. Managers seem to appreciate this sort of assistance with the difficult part of making the firm's value system operative, and secondly, they seem to be at least as satisfied with the final result of this method as with their usual ones, if not more so. If this sort of result were to be further confirmed, then we might look toward the formulating of a principle to guide in the division of labor.

> Use analysis to accept as inputs simple judgement or decisions well within a manager's experience, and to extend logically the consequences of these inputs to situations not within his experience and easy intuition.

We are suggesting with this principle that the assumption that these subtle combinations of multiple and conflicting values could only be made by experienced persons may warrant a careful examination. Perhaps they can be made with more satisfactory results using some rather simple analytical model.*

---

* Government decision-makers would undoubtedly welcome such a millenium since they are regularly faced by imponderable tradeoff decisions such as whether to invest in defence or social programs, in education or health. The editor inclines to the view that the best chance for solving problems in this area lies in a basic re-appraisal of objectives; the real question is not, How should we do things? but, What

PREDICTING POLICY CONSEQUENCES

We have remarked in our decision model on the basic human perceptual and conceptual capacity limitations, together with the often subconscious distortions which arise out of needs. These characteristics lead obviously to various degrees of selectivity and simplification when predictions must be made of the behavior of complex systems. We have suggested that these simplifications appear in management practice in the form of rules of thumb, suppression of risk, categorizing, and so on. The most obvious, and possibly the most important use of management science is to extend the volume of data and the complexity of relationships that are brought to bear on the problem of predicting policy consequences. Analysis aims here at simply enhancing the capacity of the unaided human mind. The effect then is to hold intuitive predictions up to the standards of fact and logic, testing which of the possible deficiencies in the decision process have led the manager astray in his estimate of future consequences. This is, of course, the way analysis and experiment are used in all science. They serve to police the products of unaided intuition for errors arising out of oversimplification, faulty logic, or wishful thinking. The especially important contribution of management science is to attempt this examination before the products of the manager's intuition are translated into actual policy changes for the firm. It aims to contribute as much as possible in the way of testing policies before the costly step of implementation.

Management science has, however, recently undertaken to go one additional step forward in the problem of enhancing predictions. The many years of experience and subtle insights of the manager are possibly one of the greatest

---

are we trying to do and why? If the various political and social philosophies could be surmounted to find a rational answer to this question, then suitable cost-effective methodology would probably present itself to reduce the effort of value judgements.

assets which the organization has. There is a tradition of leaving these judgements implicit, supplying the manager with the data and analysis resulting from the management scientist's efforts, but leaving it to the manager to 'integrate' this with his own thinking. This, again, is sometimes a particularly difficult thing to do. What weight to give to experience and what to the management scientist's report? If, however, the judgements and opinions of the manager could be made explicit, the notions of subjective probability and Bayesian decision now offer at least the possibility of assistance with this problem of integration. (4) The same general principle appears to apply as did in the case of goal setting. The manager might be encouraged to make his experience explicit in terms of some simple decisions well within his experience. Analysis can then be used to extend these opinions to complex situations beyond his experience, and to offer some logical guidance as to how data and opinion ought to be combined. This notion leads directly to the problem of learning effectively from experience.

LEARNING FROM EXPERIENCE

Recently a number of experiments have been carried out in which subjects were asked to make a simple decision of some sort in the face of some uncertainty. They were then offered the opportunity to 'buy' various types and quantities of information which was relevant to the decision. A large portion of the subjects in such experiments seemed to pay more for the information than was reasonable and once given some information, failed to use it as effectively as they reasonably might have. One must be careful to explain what is meant by 'reasonably' here. Suppose the subject has certain initial opinions which reflect his uncertainty as the decision is first posed to him. Suppose further that he agrees he would like to behave in ways which are consistent both with his initial opinions and with the logic of probability theory. Then it turns out that the behavior of most subjects does not meet these standards of consistency. Further, the deviations from these standards are predominantly in the direction of overpaying, overbuying, or underutilizing information.

If these should turn out to be something like fundamental human characteristics, then the role of management science could move importantly toward the improvement of the process of learning or assimilating experience. Here again, the principle would be the same. If the manager could make his opinions and values explicit in simple decisions well within his experience, a logical extension of the consequences of these could be made to more complex situations not within his experience. If this were to occur, it would generally have the effect of making the methods by which managers learn from experience more nearly like those by which scientists learn from experience. This suggests the kind of broad picture of the role of science in management which we next consider.

Chapter Six

MANAGEMENT AS EXPERIMENT

AN interesting overview or model of management for our purposes is one which regards it as a learning process involving steps such as:

1. Recognizing and conceptualizing a management decision problem, using both past experience and available data.
2. Making and implementing the decision.
3. Learning from the results of the decision how it should be modified and adding these results to the reservoir of experience on which future decisions may draw.

The process is thus one of deciding, acting, and learning from the resulting experience how to act more effectively in the future. It pictures management as a dynamic process and suggests that we might regard management as the mechanism by which organizational learning takes place. It is the adaptive mechanism by which the firm continually readjusts itself, seeking an effective relationship with its environment. It is not difficult, however, to picture science as essentially a learning process as well. The names for the steps may differ but the process is essentially the same.

Science, like management, is a diverse, complex activity and any attempt to conceptualize it must admit to producing a simplified rendering of its nature. Yet it is useful to suggest that the work of the scientist is that of:

1. Raising interesting hypotheses on the basis of both his own personal experience and intuition and the accumulated public knowledge of his discipline.

2. Designing experiments which test these hypotheses.
3. Assimilating the results both into his personal experience and the body of his discipline, thus preparing the way for new hypotheses and new experiments.

There may be some phenomena about which the scientist feels little uncertainty and thus little need for further hypothesizing and experimentation. Others, however, are matters of considerable uncertainty and thus become the subjects of extensive programs of experimentation and learning.

Viewed in this way, it may be reasonable to think of science and management as sharing certain broad common features as learning processes. If we regard a manager's conceptualization of a decision problem as a hypothesis, then his activities which are aimed at testing the validity of the hypothesis may well be regarded as experiments. Management, like science, might be seen as a dynamic, experimental, self-correcting activity, involved essentially in the task of learning. One must be careful, however, to learn what is useful from such similarities without pressing them too far. There are interesting differences in the ways in which the two learning processes are carried on. These differences appear, from this viewpoint, to be matters of degree and not matters of principle.

1. Explicit Use of the Hypothetico-Deductive Method

Since the time of Newton, physics has expressed its hypotheses and theories in mathematical language. This has the distinct advantage of permitting one to explore the deductive consequences of a hypothesis, the relations among hypotheses, and to work toward a unified theory in which everything of interest could be deduced from a small number of basic laws. Economics and, more recently, psychology and sociology have begun to emulate physics in their use of mathematical formulations of models.

If the experimental data one has in hand can be deduced from the model, if one can reach the same conclusions both deductively and experimentally, then it is said that the model 'explains' the data. The data in turn lend credence to the model, although they do not unequivocally establish its truth. Regardless of how much data is obtained, some uncertainty remains about the validity of the model in the future. Nevertheless, there comes a point at which uncertainty about the model is limited and one feels confident in using it as a prediction of what will happen in future experiments. Agreement between the model and the evidence is not a trivial matter to decide and confronts the scientist with his most difficult decisions.

This learning process, which aims at both explaining and predicting, is the hypothetico-deductive method. Of course, there has been nothing in management to compare with the well-developed mathematical theory which physics has produced. Yet it is the basic proposal of Management Science that management phenomena can be usefully captured in mathematical models and that the resulting deductive capability can be of considerable consequence for the learning process of managers. Sufficient progress has been made to create a justifiable optimism on the part of Management Scientists that this hypothesis will be progressively confirmed, and to moderate some of the scepticism of experienced managers.

2. Experiment and Experience

Learning by experience on the job has been the traditional method of increasing one's appreciation of the intricacies of management phenomena. In science, however, the tradition of learning is by means of deliberate, carefully designed experiments. This distinction between casual experience and careful experiment is a basic one. What we are proposing is that we begin the transformation of the loose informality of management experience toward the designed experience or considered experiment of science.

Experimental design requires operational definitions of the concepts involved in one's hypotheses. If we are to talk of employee morale, customer satisfaction, military worth, or a fair day's work, we must be able to say explicitly how each of these concepts is to be identified in our experience and measured. This, of course, does not always mean precise measurement in the tradition of physics. For some purposes it may be very useful to be able to distinguish operationally between high morale and low morale groups of employees, but there may be no particular need to scale morale through the assignment of a numerical value.

Experimentation implies also a specific statement of one's beliefs prior to the experiment and an explicit examination of the impact of the evidence on these beliefs. Without these, science would be a mere accumulation of observations. With them, science can attempt to wring the maximum amount of information from any body of data. In this sense, experiment tries to use data efficiently, while casual experience may use them wastefully or unreasonably. Beyond the production of its marketable goods and services, the second most important output of a firm is likely to be information on how to improve its own operations. In moving from experience toward experiment, we hope to move toward optimizing the production of this second output.

3. The Uses of Intuition

Yet there is a major difference in the ultimate reliance placed upon intuitive decision-making by scientists as opposed to managers. In management decision-making one is often required to place final reliance on intuitive processes and to evaluate managers on their intuitive skills alone. Lacking any well-developed alternatives, pressed by the ongoing affairs of the firm, and taking considerable pride in 'managerial judgement', managers are content to leave their decision processes on an intuitive level.

The scientist, however, makes full use of his intuition to reach conclusions, make discoveries, and raise hypotheses, but does not finally rely on intuition alone. Indeed, the meaning of 'objectivity' in science is not that intuition is bad, but that it must be checked by logic and experiment.

After having reached a tentative conclusion, the scientist undertakes to test it by logical deduction and experimental inference. Science as an activity may be roughly divided into the largely intuitive process of discovering and the formal process of justifying one's discoveries. For the scientist, intuition, however valuable, is not to be trusted, but tested.

4. The Pressure of Affairs

It is the very nature of management that it involves decision-making in the context of rapidly moving events. Opportunities must be grasped or they are lost, situations demand quick responses, and the size and complexity of his job strains the cognitive ability of the typical manager. The scientist, however, often finds himself working in a context which does not demand quick decisions and fast reactions, which permits thoughtful and deliberate progress toward a conclusion, and assures a considerable freedom from distractions.

It is manifestly nonsense to propose anything to the manager which does not recognize clearly the pressures under which he must operate. It would be useless to suggest that the manager ought to behave as though he worked in the context of the stereotypic scientist, when in fact he does not. A further basic hypothesis of Management Science is that it can improve the learning-decision-making process within the constraints of the management environment, not simply by denying these constraints. Thus the problem is how to optimize learning given the costs of getting information, the information-handling capacities, and the time deadlines which characterize the management situation. Perhaps this sensitivity to the 'realities' of management decision-making is one of the fundamentally distinctive features of Management Science. It is worth emphasizing again that these distinctions between management and science are matters of degree and not of principle. Managers and scientists differ, generally speaking, in the degree to which their hypotheses are mathematically expressed, the extent to which their experience is carefully designed, the amount of their final reliance on intuition, and the degree to which the pressure of affairs forces their decision-making. Management Science might be thought of as the program of reducing the degree to which management and science differ in an effort to enhance the effectiveness of management.

THE BASIC PROPOSAL OF MANAGEMENT SCIENCE

Our basic hypothesis is thus that things will improve if the methods of science are applied to the decisions which managers must make, that something is to be gained by making the learning-adaptive processes of management more nearly like those of science. We do not propose that the manager become fully involved in the technical details of science, but rather that he adopt its strategy while delegating some of the tactical details to the trained Management Scientist.

Management Science proposes to take seriously the task of giving explicit, reasonable answers to such questions as:

1. When should a manager rely on his intuition in making a decision and when should he try to become very explicit and experimental about it? Clearly, not every decision will reasonably be subjected to a fully deliberated analysis.
2. When should the manager delegate a part of his learning process to a Management Scientist, to another manager, or to a digital computer? Our basic aim is to show that he can delegate some tasks, thus giving himself more time to perform those for which he himself is uniquely qualified.
3. How prolonged should be the process of search for alternative courses of action? How much data should be obtained in predicting their consequences? How may these data be reasonably assimilated into one's

experience? What predictions, inferences, or forecasts are reasonable in view of both data and experience?

In short, Management Science aims at optimizing the learning-adaptation process. It seeks to do this within the constraints and pressures of the ongoing affairs of the managerial situation. It seeks further, to make full use of the most valuable asset in any decision situation, the rich experience and insight of managers themselves.

REFERENCES

1. Drury, H. B., *Scientific Management – A History and Criticism*. New York; Columbia University Press, 1922.

2. Fishburn, Peter C., *Decision and Value Theory*. New York; John Wiley and Sons, Inc., 1964.

3. Shelly, Maynard W. and Glenn L. Bryan (eds.), *Human Judgements and Optimality*. New York; John Wiley and Sons Inc., 1964.

4. Schlaifer, Robert, *Introduction to Statistics for Business Decisions*. New York: McGraw-Hill Book Co., Inc., 1961.

Part II

QUANTITATIVE
DECISION-MAKING

Harold Bierman, Jr

Professor of Accounting and Managerial Economics,
Graduate School of Business and Public Administration,
Cornell University

Hal Bierman graduated during his naval service in 1945, and is a veteran of World War II and of the Korean War. His MBA and PhD were obtained at the University of Michigan. He had previously been on the staff at Louisiana State University, Michigan University and Chicago University before joining Cornell in 1956.

He is a popular and experienced teacher and is a member of the Cornell Executive Development Program. He has been associated with the University of the West Indies since 1964 and was Visiting Professor of Management there 1965–66. He has also visited England to lecture on Investment and Managerial Accounting.

Widely experienced in industrial consultancy, Hal Bierman has had service with Boeing, Ford, Shell, Arthur Young. His honours include being Vice-President of the American Accounting Association, and his articles on financial administration are legion.

The books he has written include:

Managerial Accounting, An Introduction (Collier-Macmillan, 1959).

The Capital Budgeting Decision (with S. Smidt, 1960; rev. ed., Macmillan, N.Y., 1966)

Quantitative Analysis for Business Decisions (with L. Fouraker and R. K. Jaedicke, 1961; rev. ed. with C. P. Bonini, Richard D. Irwin Inc., 1965).

Management Decisions for Cash and Marketable Securities (with Alan McAdams, Collier-Macmillan, 1962).

Topics in Cost Accounting and Decisions (McGraw-Hill, 1963).

Financial and Managerial Accounting (Macmillan, N.Y., 1963).

Financial Accounting Theory (Macmillan, N.Y., 1965).

Financial Accounting; An Introduction (with Allan Drebin, Collier-Macmillan, 1968).

Managerial Accounting (with Allan Drebin, Collier-Macmillan, 1968).

INTRODUCTION

It would be naïve to set a date and state that the birth of quantitative decision-making occurred on that date. Long ago a Stone-Age man saw a bevy of dinosaurs and concluded that he should go in the opposite direction. His decision was empirical, analytical, and quantitative.*

Businessmen have been putting numbers together for the purposes of decision-making for centuries. While we can agree that quantitative approaches to decision-making are not a recent discovery, it is also true that several developments have accelerated the rate of usage of quantitative methods. For example, consider the advent of the electronic computer, the entry of mathematically-trained technicians into business decision-making resulting in the development of such techniques as linear and non-linear programming, inventory and queueing models, and the splitting off from classical statistics of a body of knowledge called modern statistical decision theory. The list could be made much longer but the above give an indication of why many would say there has been a revolution in the art of decision-making in recent years.

This part of the book is divided into three to discuss:
(a) the nature of decision-making with special attention to quantitative aspects of decisions,

---

* It would not only be naïve: it would be grotesquely anachronistic by the few hundred million years which separated Stone-Age man from the dinosaur. However, the editor has overlooked this slight error since Professor Bierman's sense of *future* time is much more dependable and germane to this subject.

(*b*) the future of quantitative decision-making, followed by a chapter containing a technical note,

(*c*) decision-making under uncertainty where time is a factor.

Chapter Seven

THE NATURE OF DECISION-MAKING

IT comes as no surprise that man makes decisions and that some men make good decisions without the aid of books and courses of study in decision-making. Why study the subject of decision-making? In fact why study any subject? You should remember that long ago there was an ancestor of yours, with a native intelligence that matched yours, who did know of the wheel. That which is a brilliant innovation, a result of rare genius, becomes available to great numbers of lesser intellects through the interpretative mediums of books and teachers. Hopefully by studying decision-making we can increase the likelihood of making 'good' decisions. We can improve decision-making by improving our general understanding and approach to the decision process and secondly by improving our techniques for approaching specific decisions. We want to have a decision process which is 'most effective' and likely to lead to decisions that are consistent with the goals of the organization. Why do we not choose *the* correct decision? Given a suitably powerful forecasting device (always correct in its prognostications) we could make many more correct decisions, but unfortunately our ability to forecast the future is very limited.

Decisions may be classified in numerous ways. First let us consider the frequency of the decision, and divide all decisions into:

(*a*) a unique one-time decision,
(*b*) a repetitive decision with either reasonably constant or randomly-spaced time between decisions.

Most unique one-shot decisions are convertible into randomly-spaced decisions; however it is still true that there are many decisions which most of us make once (though some make once several times). For example, we choose one undergraduate college and one wife. A firm may choose a plant site or a new executive vice-president. Those are important decisions and despite the fact that we may make the decision only once we may choose to spend considerable time and effort in making the decisions because of their importance.

Most decisions are repetitive and fortunately the store of information we gather for making the previous decisions may be carried forward and applied to the decisions coming up. Complex decisions become routine through familiarity. A New Yorker of average intelligence can choose the correct subway; a visitor of superior intelligence is apt to head off in the wrong direction. The computation of the yield of an investment and the application of a simple decision rule is a complex task for a clerk the first time he approaches the problem. After the fiftieth computation an adventuresome clerk is likely to complain of his routine work load (if he complains sufficiently the task will be given to a computer).

It is very helpful when we can move a decision from the unique classification to the repetitive classification for then there is a possibility that we can effectively use information accumulated from past similar decisions. Hopefully we can routinize the decision. However not all repetitive decisions can be made routine. Repetitive decisions may be classified as to whether or not each decision is unique in some manner. We can imagine a continuous spectrum measuring the different degrees of uniqueness of decisions. The subway decision for the New Yorker going to work is an example of a relatively homogeneous set of repetitive decisions (assuming no special trips requiring special travel plans). A business manager establishing decision rules for ordering pencils is faced with this same type of repetitive decision.

On the other hand, there are many decisions which though

repetitive are each a little (or greatly) different from previous decisions. Hiring of personnel for managerial jobs or promoting individuals are examples of repetitive but different decisions.

Decisions may also be classified as to the degree of importance of the outcomes. If the future existence of the firm hinges on the outcome of the decision, this decision will receive a different degree of consideration than if the decision is apt to affect the level of profit by some amount, say a ·001 deviation from the expected profit.

Fortunately for our mental health most decisions we make are not of crucial importance, i.e. no matter how the decisions turn out the organization will survive and the decision-maker will survive also.

Placing the decision in perspective is extremely important. Taking a broad point of view, how important is the decision? Is it worthy of the effort being devoted to its resolution? In technical language, 'What is the value of additional information?'

There is another important characteristic of decision-making. We may make an incorrect decision and make it correctly, or we can make a correct decision for all the wrong reasons. We may decide incorrectly and arbitrarily not to promote Mr Jones who may then move on to a better job, and we may replace him with a man who is not qualified using any known standard but turns out to be outstanding.* Because of random events a well-made and well-researched decision may turn out to be incorrect.

While some persons have difficulty reaching decisions, in

* Personnel selection leaves scope for much improvement. There is yet no known test which is entirely successful to sift out schoolchildren, university students, marriage partners or executives (in spite of the notoriously high fees which companies are prepared to pay to personnel consultants for the latter service). Selection has so far been fairly intransigent to management science though multi-characteristic analysis may eventually prove successful once the normative measures really do represent the standard situation at issue. Too often we fail to realize what characteristics are needed for the *job* though we may effectively appraise the man.

general, mankind is blessed with a characteristic of being able to reach a decision. Your very presence on this earth and your ability to read this book indicates that your ancestors made some pretty fair decisions in the past.

Frequently a decision is an instant reaction which is more an impulse or an instinctive action rather than a conscious decision. Or the decision may be the result of national or world affairs (such as the potato famine in Ireland or one of the many persecutions which drove this or that group from Europe). While the decision-maker thought he was making a decision, the historian may conclude that the individual was merely caught in the stream of events. But too much can be made of this interpretation of man's progress. Man does have opportunity to make choices and those who are slow to make decisions or tend to make the incorrect decision pay a price.

To this point the differences of different types of decisions have been stressed. Now let us consider some common elements of making decisions. All decisions have four elements. We shall discuss three of these elements, and then introduce the fourth element after investigating an example.

1. The possible actions we may take. For example in the context of an inventory problem, the possible actions would be the different possible order sizes ranging fron zero to n, where n may be a large number.
2. The possible states of nature which may occur. One of the possible states will be the true state. For example, continuing the inventory example, the possible states of nature are that the demand for the product will be $0, 1, 2, \ldots, n$. After the period has ended we will be able to say that demand was x units. Before the period has ended we can weight each event by the likelihood of its occurrence, that is, by the probabilities of the various states of nature being true.
3. For each act and each state of nature there is a consequence. For example, we could order zero units in which case we will have zero profits for all possible

demands. If we order one unit and demand is one we would have some amount of profit. If demand were larger than one and if we ordered one we would have less profit than it was possible to attain with a different ordering policy.

The following example involving an inventory type problem illustrates the general procedure for approaching a decision. We will use a conditional profit table. Across the top of the table will be a complete description of the reasonable acts or decisions which may be chosen by the decision maker (we normally will not list obviously undesirable decisions). Down the side of the table are listed the possible states of nature or possible events which occur. In the body of the table are the conditional profits (or costs or values). We define the entries as being conditional profits since they depend on the act which is decided on and the state of nature (or event) that actually occurs. Initially we shall assume that we are able to measure the consequences in units of money. Later we shall refine this assumption.

Past experience (and expectations of the future) indicate that the demand for a product will have the following probability distribution:

Demand	Probability of Demand
0	·50
1	·40
2	·10
3	·00
	———
	1·00

We can order any integer amount, but we cannot reorder. The cost of a unit of product is $4, the selling price $10. If the unit is not sold during the period it has no value. For each unit sold there is a profit of $6. For each unit purchased but unsold there is a loss of $4. Losses are

represented as negative profits and the conditional profit
table is:

States Acts	Order: 0	1	2
0	0	−4	−8
1	0	6	2
2	0	6	12
Expected Profit	0	1·00	−2·00

In the bottom line of the table is the expected profit of
each act. These were computed as follows:

Act: Order 1

State	1 Prob.		2 Profits for Act: Order 1		3 Col. 1 × Col 2
0	·50	×	−4	=	−2·00
1	·40	×	6	=	2·40
2	·10	×	6	=	·60
	1·00		Expected profit		1·00

Act: Order 2

State	1 Prob.	2 Profits for Act: Order 2	3 Col. 1 × Col. 2
0	·50	−8	−4·00
1	·40	2	·80
2	·10	12	1·20
	1·00	Expected profit	−2·00

Comparison of the expected profits (the last line of the
table) may be interpreted to mean that we should order one
unit since that act has the highest expected profit. We would
not order two units since the expected profit of that act is
less than either ordering no units or ordering one unit.

In most situations this approach to solving inventory
problems would result in a great deal of arithmetic. Fortunately there are techniques which can be used that bypass
the use of the conditional table but that retain the basic

approach to the problem. The amount of arithmetic is no problem when these techniques are used.

However, there remains a basic problem. Inspection of the conditional profit table shows that if we order one unit there is a ·5 probability of a loss of $4. (i.e. when demand is zero.) Now assume that the numbers in the table represent millions of dollars. Is the best decision still to order one unit? Can we accept a ·5 probability of a loss of four million dollars? The decision rule we used to this point was 'compute the expected monetary value of each act and choose that act which has the highest expected profit or the lowest expected cost'. But it may not be appropriate to use this rule. The consequences resulting from the occurrence of a state of nature may be so undesirable or of such limited use that we cannot just take a weighted average of the possible dollar outcomes to reach a decision.

One possibility is to find a different decision rule. Some decision-makers prefer the 'Minimax' decision rule.* The minimax rule says to find that act which has the minimum maximum cost. The maximum cost or negative profit of ordering zero units is $0, of ordering 1 unit is $4, of ordering 2 units is $8. The act with the minimum maximum cost is 'order zero'. How reasonable is it to follow a minimax decision rule? Imagine a situation where the probability of demand being zero is ·001 and demand being one is ·999. Would the decision to order zero units still seem reasonable? It is still the minimax decision, but it does not seem to be reasonable in view of the small probability of the 'demand is zero' event occurring.

We are now able to list the fourth element of decision making:

4. Establish a criterion (or several criteria) which will enable us to choose the best of the several eligible acts.

* A more comprehensive but simple guide to other classical decision rules such as 'regret', 'optimism', 'pessimism' and 'rationality' is given by D. W. Miller and M. K. Starr, *Executive Decisions and Operations Research*, ch. 5 (Prentice-Hall, 1960).

Initially we computed the expected profit and chose the optimum act based on this expectation. Secondly, the minimax criterion was applied, and this led to a different decision. We are not limited to these two choices (these are two of the most interesting alternatives).

One confusion about the minimax decision criterion is that in a special type of situation (a two-person-zero-sum game), with specified assumptions concerning the rationality of the opponents we can make statements about the desirability of a minimax strategy. In a game (or situation) involving nature, where silly old nature may not be rational, minimax is not a very good general criterion. While it may accidentally lead to a good decision (by good we mean consistent with some undefined criterion), this is not a sufficient characteristic to recommend it to our decision-makers in the real world. At this point we suggest that you accept the criterion of computing the expected value and choosing that act with the highest expected value. However, when we defined the units in the profit table as being in millions of dollars the use of expected value is not necessarily consistent with your intuitive preference. One of the difficulties is in the use of dollars to measure the amounts of benefits or costs which result from a set of acts and states.

Assume that there are two investments under consideration. With investment A you receive $\$X$ for certain. With investment B you have a ·5 probability of receiving $1,000 and a ·5 probability of receiving $0. What does the value of X have to be for you to be indifferent between the two investments? On an expected monetary value basis your answer would be $500, but most persons would answer differently.* Now, let us ask a slightly different question. How much would you pay for the privilege of undertaking investment B? Again the answer on an expected monetary

* It would depend on how they see the usefulness of $1,000 or $0 to themselves and on the current state of their finances to make the investment. For further exposition of these ideas see R. Schlaifer, *Probability and Statistics for Business Decisions*, ch. 2 (McGraw-Hill, 1959).

value basis would be $500, but most of us would not write a check for $500 to pay for the investment.

The above examples indicate that it may not be appropriate to use the monetary expectations as the basis for decision-making. But there is an even more dramatic example (the following is called the St Petersburg Paradox).

Assume a situation where a fair coin is to be tossed a number of times and the amount you are to be given is equal to 2^n where n is the number of the toss on which the first head appears. The schedule of your possible winnings is as follows:

Number of tosses for first head	Winnings
1	$ 2
2	4
3	8
4	16
.	.
.	.
.	.
n	2^n

How much would you pay to play this game? It is interesting that if we multiply the 'winnings' by the probability of each event, and sum the products we find that the expected monetary value of the game is an infinite amount. But the average person would pay considerably less than twenty dollars to play. To make the above example even more striking we will change the winnings to 2^n pennies. The expected monetary value remains an infinite amount, but if we were willing to pay twenty dollars previously, the amount we would invest now is considerably less.

If we cannot use expected value of dollars in making decisions, what is an alternative? In 1944 a book *Theory of Games and Economic Behavior* by John Von Neumann and Oskar Morgenstern was published. The work introduced concepts which are very important to decision-making; among them is the so-called concept of modern utility. By investigating a person's reactions to decisions involving risk, a relationship is obtained which enables us to convert the consequences of an act and state from dollars to another measure which is called utility. If you were willing to pay $100 for the investment *B* described previously (·5 probability of winning $1,000 and ·5 probability of winning $0) we would say that the utility of $100 was equal to the utility of the investment.

An important lesson to be learned is that it may be misleading to make decisions based on monetary expectations, and that we are led into the use of utility in analysing the desirability of a set of decisions. A reasonable procedure is to take the expectations of the utilities of different events and compute the expected utility of each act.* The act with the greatest expected utility would be the optimum act. This procedure is called the 'Bayes Decision Rule' and was first introduced by Thomas Bayes in a paper titled 'An Essay Toward Solving a Problem in the Doctrine of Chance' published in 1763.

This last reference leads us to the very interesting area which is called statistical decision theory.† Statistical decision theory relates to the problem of obtaining information about which state of nature is true, using evidence to adjust the probability distribution of the states of nature to arrive at new probabilities, and finally, taking into consideration the possible losses (or costs or profits) associated with each act, choose the optimum act.‡

What are the possible applications of the above techniques? Almost all decisions are made under conditions of uncertainty, thus the applications are extensive. The following business decisions may make use of the concepts discussed in this section:

* *op. cit.*, Schlaifer, ch. 2.

† This subject has been extensively covered by P. C. Fishburn, *Decision and Value Theory* (Wiley, 1964) and by W. T. Morris, *Management Science: A Bayesian Introduction* (Prentice-Hall, 1968).

‡ These ideas are more fully developed by Ray Cuninghame-Green in Part IV.

(a) inventory control decisions
(b) cost-price-volume decisions (including break-even analysis)
(c) insurance decisions
(d) capital investment decisions
(e) credit decisions
(f) marketable security decisions
(g) issue of debt or stock decisions
(h) marketing decisions

But the prime importance of the techniques discussed are not necessarily in formal application in the above areas. Rather the primary benefit may be a general method of approaching a decision and as a tool for explaining the reasons why you reached your decision. Two perfectly reasonable persons may arrive at different decisions if they have different probability distributions associated with the possible events. Or they may have different concepts of the losses associated with the events. To a great extent these two factors explain the large amount of trading which is done on the stock exchange.

One characteristic to be remembered about all decision making is that it is possible that a correct decision (in an expected value sense) will lead to an undesirable result. For example, in the inventory example developed previously we could order 1 unit since that act has the highest expected value and not sell any units (there is a ·5 probability of demand being equal to 0). This has an important control implication. It may be more important to judge the quality of the inputs into the decision-making process and the decision-making process itself than to look at the results of the decision.* Of course it is also important to look at the

* In other words, a 'good' decision is one that has been reached by logical analysis and its 'goodness' is not to be judged by whether events prove the decision to be 'right'. Events are the result of chance; and in the long run 'good' analytical techniques of decision-making will always show worthwhile superiority over any logically inferior method simply because they deal with the elements of chance and risk more effectively than any alternative method.

results and adjust our operating procedures or our evidence-gathering procedures. However, it is suggested that the decision-maker who orders one unit and has a loss of $4 when no units are demanded may be making a better decision than the person who orders no units in the same situation, if the facts are as given in the described example.

A possible and unfortunate result of this reasonable approach to performance evaluation is that it weakens top management's ability to jump to conclusions relative to the performance of their subordinates, but this is a fact of life in the world of uncertainty, the world in which we all must operate.

Chapter Eight

THE FUTURE OF QUANTITATIVE
DECISION-MAKING

IN general, forecasting is a risky art. In this section my forecast of the future of quantitative decision-making will be of modest dimensions thus relatively safe.* I will describe known techniques and predict that they will be used increasingly by administrators. I will not attempt to predict what new techniques will be developed in the future, except to make the safe prediction that such new techniques will be developed and a student of business must be alert to their development.

Any discussion of the future must consider the impact of the electronic computer. Until recently the electronic computer was used to do the same things that businesses did previously. The computer did the tasks more rapidly, and perhaps in a slightly different manner, but they did essentially the same tasks. Thus a computer could record accounting entries without making entries to the right and left hand side of ledger accounts and underlining account balances, but basically it was doing the same thing that the bookkeeper formerly did by hand.

We are now entering a new stage of computer utilization. The computer is now doing things that previously were not done at all because it was either too expensive to do the tasks, or if the costs were not an effective restraint, the time of computation was (by the time the problem was

* At this point, readers may be tempted to recall that the previous chapter implied that the more modest, relatively safe forecast was not inevitably conclusive to the 'best' decision. Before pursuing this thought they are advised to read on.

solved it would be too late to use the solution). There is no question that the computer will be doing more and more chores previously done by people, but it is also true that the computer will give rise to the invention of new forms of information systems. Among the tasks currently being done by computers (that were previously done by people) or that we can expect to be done by computers are:

- (a) finding legal references
- (b) diagnosing an illness
- (c) solving a linear programming problem (and many other types of mathematical problems)
- (d) handling the payroll preparation
- (e) scheduling production
- (f) determining optimum inventory order points and order sizes
- (g) matching men and women for possible marriage

The above list is varied and you may not agree that the computer can do all the jobs better than chance or a person making intuitive decisions. However, each of the above tasks has certain characteristics that lend them to computer solution. There may be a large amount of computation, or solving of mathematical relationships, or a large amount of information must be remembered and matched with other information. The computer can do these jobs very efficiently.

As an example of the sort of thing that would not be undertaken at all, if it were not for the availability of a computer, consider the simulation of the economy and the effects of changing conditions on an oil company. The economy being simulated may be that of the world if we are dealing with a corporation operating throughout the world. This sort of exercise may not be feasible if done by hand, but a computer can handle a problem with many times the amount of complexities that can be done by hand.

In the future we can expect to have computer consoles in the offices of top middle managers and the mode of conversation between the manager and the machine will be plain

English (with strict rules of grammar). The manager will ask for information or for the solution of a problem, and the computer will give a nearly instantaneous solution (and may charge the manager a toll for the effort).

The decision that results may not be any different than that resulting from the manager approaching the problem from an intuitive point of view, but since the decision will be based on more information somewhat better analysed, we would expect the manager of the future to be correct a higher percentage of the time, than he is currently.

The above forecast is not really very bold since the technology is already available and by the time this book is published there will be firms doing exactly as described.

What does the future hold in store? In the area of the computer and its applications I hesitate to make predictions. Predictions made by experts in the past have fallen very short of the mark. The actual extent of use, and the capability of the current machines, have exceeded expectations. It is apparent that in any process where well-defined directions are given, where quick or complex computations are made, where memory is required, where associations of two or more variables have to be made, that the computer will be a tough contender to beat.

THE DEVELOPMENT OF MATHEMATICAL MODELS

A computer does what it is told. If it is solving an inventory problem it needs an inventory model. Supplying the appropriate model is the task of the operations researcher or the management science expert (the terms management science and operations research may be used interchangeably).*

Mathematical models may be used to help make decisions in a wide range of human endeavor, and we are still in our

* This is using the words management science rather loosely and not in the same exact sense as developed by William T. Morris in Part I. There are sufficient obvious examples of persons who are operations researchers but not management scientists to readily prove the point.

infancy in terms of developing these models. For example, in the area of inventory management there has been a veritable explosion of knowledge since 1953. Recent quantitative analysis journals have carried many articles dealing with additional refinements to known inventory models. The same is true with queueing theory and with mathematical programming. Currently, in many areas of decision making there are known complex mathematical models that have not yet been fully digested by managers. The state of the act of application is lagging the development of the theoretical models. We can expect the development of further mathematical models to an increasingly large number of diverse problems. In the past most of the applications have been in the area of production and the control of operations. Recently the use of normative models has spread to the areas of marketing and finance. We can also expect to see a wider use in the large range planning (or policy) areas.* Within the next few years you can expect to see mathematical models (frequently combined with the use of an electronic computer) applied to a wide range of managerial problems. Problems that one conventionally thinks require experience and judgement will be broken down into their basic components and the inputs of experience and judgements will be systematically incorporated into their model. Rather than being the basis of the decision, these factors will become inputs that will influence the decision, but will not by themselves decide the decision. The question 'why?' will be asked more and more, and a large group of executives will want a better answer than 'that is the way we have done it in the past'.

To manage effectively the manager of the future will have to understand the mathematical model being used in order to understand the limitations of the model. A prime danger of the managerial situation that will develop in the future is that only a few persons will understand the model being used, and they will be able to introduce bias into the deci-

* This will be particularly true for manpower planning, corporate planning, industry-wide planning, and national economic planning.

sions, without the bias being identified as being present or its nature disclosed. Presently the ignorance of a decision-maker becomes readily apparent if he is ignorant as he explains his reasoning. In the future a mathematical model builder may choose not to explain his model in an intelligible manner, but may merely choose to overwhelm his colleagues with the complexity of his model.

It should be understood that any model is an abstraction from reality and generally simplifies the real world. The nature of the simplifications should be clearly understood since it is possible to leave out the relevant variables in order to be able to solve the problem. It is very easy to choose a nice problem that can be solved, rather than a nasty problem for which there is no solution, even though only the solution to the nasty problem has any relevance to a real decision.

The job of the manager in the future will actually be much more complex than it is currently. In the past a decision maker could use his intuition and imperfect information and not be criticized since that was all he had available for making the decision. Now and in the future more sophisticated tools will be available. But unfortunately these are sensitive fragile tools and require expert use. The seemingly exact answers produced by a mathematical model may be misleading. For example, in a linear programming type of situation with four constraints (four factors of production are limiting production), the optimum solution will involve no more than four products. This solution could be a great shock to a firm that is currently producing a product line involving 100 different items. The manager that took the linear programming solution and applied it might well find himself out of a job. The difficulty in this particular situation is that probably the firm cannot sell all the units it can produce at a given price. Thus the revenue relationship is not constant and the objective (or profit) function is not linear and we should have used a different model (a non-linear profit function). Or it may be that we expressed four constraints mathematically, but there are actually more than four constraints though some of them are difficult to express mathematically. In any event, it is apparent that the manager of the future will receive information from operations researchers that will require interpretation before the instructions are exercised. The assumption underlying the model must be understood.*

DECISION THEORY

Modern statistical decision theory has given business decision makers the tools they need for being able to incorporate attitudes about the uncertain future into decisions.

We first discuss a situation where we start from a position, obtain more information and then revise our initial position based on the additional information. In fact, before obtaining the information we will compare the cost of obtaining the information with the expected value of the information, to determine if we want to buy the information.

Example
Assume that a card is going to be drawn from a deck. If it is a spade I win $1,000. The decision will be based on expected monetary value.

If it is any of the other three suits I lose $200, but I can decide not to bet. Since there is one chance in four of winning $1,000 (an expected value of $250), and three chances in four of losing $200 (an expected value of $150) I decided to engage in the gamble because the expected monetary value (EMV) is thus $250 − $150 = $100.

Now suppose a third party offers to peek and tell me the card before I have to bet, and assume that the process is legal and moral. What is the expected value of the information?

The tree diagram shown in Figure 1 shows this new situation.

* The communication difficulties of this situation will ease as operations researchers become promoted from services to line management. One might then expect management to couch its problems in more sophisticated terms and to readily understand the more easily implementable reports and recommendations.

The path 'buy information' has a higher expected monetary value than the path 'do not buy information'. As a result of buying the information, the increase in the expected value is $150 and if the information costs some amount less than $150 then I would be willing to buy the information (thus eliminating the possibility of losing $200).

It may be that my informant can only tell me that the card has a black suit if a club or spade is drawn. This would be imperfect information and I would pay less than $150

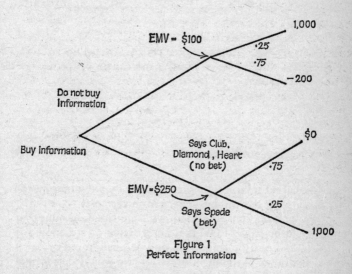

Figure 1
Perfect Information

for this information. Assuming the card is replaced in the deck, the probability of winning will be ·5 if my friend tells me the suit is black. The value of this information is somewhat more difficult to compute than in the previous example. We can again use a decision tree to illustrate the problem at issue (see Figure 2).

The expected monetary value of the 'buy information'

path is $200 and this is an improvement over the no information path of $100.* We would be willing to pay up to $100 for this imperfect information (we had been willing to pay $150 for perfect information).

The example is artificially simple but it does illustrate the basic problem involving the opportunity to purchase

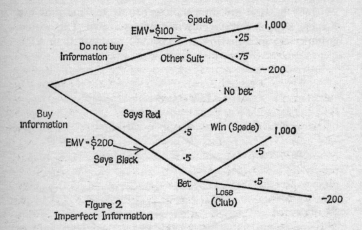

Figure 2
Imperfect Information

additional information by sampling, or by any other means of finding out more about the decision variables.

In some situations information has no value. Assume that we would be paid $1,000 if either a spade or a diamond is drawn, and our informant can only tell us if a red or black card is drawn. Without information we would decide that betting was desirable. With the information that the card was red (or that the card was black) we would also bet. The information would not change our decision so it has no

---

* The $200 is composed of the probabilities of black and spade multiplied by the potential winnings ($0.5 \times 0.5 \times \$1,000 = \$250$) minus the probabilities of black and club multiplied by the potential loss ($0.5 \times 0.5 \times \$200 = \$50$). The $100 may be derived in like manner. For other examples of the value of perfect information see Slonim (ed. Yewdall) *op. cit.*, ch. 18, and ch. 14 below.

value to us. The fact that information may have no value should be kept in mind. Sometimes there is a tendency to accumulate information where we already have enough information to make the decision, and no information that is available is going to change our decision.

Real life examples are much more complex than that of the illustrations. We could move from a situation where only a few possible events may occur to the situation where a very large number of events might occur (in fact we can assume an infinite number of possibilities and move to the use of a continuous probability distribution).

In the future we can expect a much wider use of the type of analysis presented here. Take any situation where you start from a position and can modify it with new information. This could be a doctor diagnosing a patient, or a marketing vice-president trying to decide whether or not to market a new product.*

Perhaps the most important of applications of decision theory involves the taking of an expectation, that is, multiplying the consequences of an act and event by the probability of the event and summing for all possible events. We have been using expected monetary value in this section to compute the value of the information, but as has been explained previously, the use of money may not be appropriate. We can switch to the case of utility measures (or other techniques) if that is appropriate. The process of incorporating all possible events and all possible consequences in a systematic manner is extremely useful. Secondly, the realization that the decision may not be made using the monetary expectations is also extremely important. We may want to consider an investment as being eligible if it has a positive expected present value, but that might not be sufficient justification for saying that it should be undertaken. In fact in some situations we might be pleased to accept investments with a negative expected monetary

* The application of this type of analysis to marketing is well treated by W. Alderson and P. E. Green, *Planning and Problem Solving in Marketing* (Irwin, 1964).

value; for example, insurance may be desirable despite the fact that it may have a negative expected value.*

* The theme of investment is considered by George A. Taylor in Part III.

Chapter Nine

A TECHNICAL NOTE ON DECISION-MAKING WITH UNCERTAINTY WHERE TIME IS A FACTOR

WE have already discussed decision making under uncertainty in several contexts. In this section we shall consider the interaction of uncertainty and the necessity of taking the timing of the benefits or outlays into consideration as they affect the investor's outlook. In practice we would not only have to consider uncertainty but also the time value of money: however, the time value of money is dealt with in Part III of this book so the examples that follow assume a time discount rate of 0%. This enables attention to be focused more rigorously upon the theme of utility in decision-making. In the example that follows we shall use an assumed utility function to illustrate several possible approaches to solving the problem.

Assume there are two sequential and identical lotteries separated by one time period. If one lottery is undertaken the second has to be undertaken also.

Period 1
·5 probability of $0 and ·5 probability of $1,000.

Period 2
·5 probability of $0 and ·5 probability of $1,000. The following utility function applies to the decision-maker.

Dollars	Utility
$	U($)
−400	−60
−200	−50

Dollars	Utility
$	$U(\$)$
−50	−49·8
0	0
100	20
200	25
300	40
600	46
800	48
950	49·8
1,000	50
1,200	52
1,600	56
2,000	60

Solution 1 – Incorrect

Compute the expected utility of the lottery of each period. Add the expected utilities to obtain the expected utility of the investment. Find the certainty equivalent for that utility.

Time Period

1      $E_1(U) = (0·5 \times 0) + (0·5 \times 50) = 25$

2      $E_2(U) = (0·5 \times 0) + (0·5 \times 50) = 25$

$$E(U) = \overline{50}$$

The monetary equivalent of utility of 50 is $1,000, and this may be considered to be the certainty equivalent of the lottery.

This procedure is incorrect. It incorrectly assumed that $(UA+B) = U(A)+U(B)$, where A is the certainty equivalent of period 1 and B is the certainty equivalent of period 2.

The utility of a sum of A plus B dollars is not necessarily equal to the sum of the utility of the component A and the utility of component B.

Solution 2 – Incorrect

We could compute the utility of the lottery of each time period and then find the certainty equivalent of that lottery. By discounting these dollar amounts back to the present and then adding, we obtain the certainty equivalent of the investment. We convert an uncertain situation into a certainty equivalent expressed in terms of dollars, and then accomplish the time discounting using these dollar amounts.

The certainty equivalent of a utility measure of 25 is $200. Since the discount rate is 0%, the sum of the present values of the certainty equivalents is $400. Is this the value of the sequential lotteries?

The error in this procedure is it assumes that the utility function which applies to the second lottery is unchanged by what happens in the first lottery. It treats a $2,000 income, which results from two winnings, the same as a $1,000 income followed by a $1,000 income with the same utility function applied in both situations. However, after the first $1,000 is earned the utility function (which represents attitudes toward risk) must also change, however slight a change.*

The error introduced by the certainty equivalent approach in sequential gambles may be less substantial than errors which result from other procedures, but nevertheless the procedure is in error.

Solution 3 – Correct

Another method of describing the difficulty with Solution 2 is to state that the outcomes of the lotteries have not been described correctly. There are actually three possible outcomes $0, $1,000 and $2,000. This can be shown by the use of a decision tree. (See Figure 3.)

Event 'win $1,000' can occur in two different ways, each with a ·25 probability. We should add the probabilities associated with the event 'win $1,000' and then compute the following table:

Income	Utility of Income	Probability	Expectation
$0	0	·25	0
$1,000	50	·50	25
$2,000	60	·25	15

Expected Utility 40

* In other words, as a person obtains more money so it alters his utility preference for additional money. This is an obvious illustration of the law of diminishing marginal returns.

The monetary equivalent of a 40 utility measure is $300, thus we would be indifferent between the sequence of lotteries and $300 for certain. It should be noted that we could have redescribed the sequential lotteries into an equivalent one-shot lottery with outcomes $0, $1,000 and $2,000.

Solution 3 is a correct approach to the sequential lottery situation.

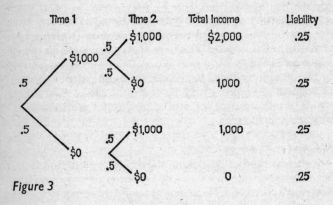

Figure 3

In the above example we found a certainty equivalent. Now consider the situation where there is an outlay of $400 required at time 0 in order to play the sequential lottery.

Solution 4 – Incorrect
We could compare 40, the utility computed above of the two lotteries, to the utility of the outlay of $400 (which is −60). We find the sum of the utilities is negative, indicating the investment is not desirable (the utility of $0 is 0, thus a negative utility indicates an undesirable investment). This procedure is not correct since it confuses an outlay of $400 with a loss of $400. Also, we are not describing the possible events correctly.

Solution 5 – Incorrect

Instead of comparing the utility of the certainty equivalent and the utility of the initial outlay we could compare the dollar amounts of the certainty equivalent and the outlay. In the above example (solution 3) the certainty equivalent of the sequential lotteries is $300 and the outlay is $400, thus we should reject the investment. It is not obvious that this is a bad procedure, though we shall see in the next solution that we should accept the investment. However, we will have to use another example to show that the procedure being described can lead to non-rational decisions.

A fault of the procedure is that the certainty equivalent of $300 for the lottery without an outlay, assumed a set of outcomes which are changed as soon as there is a required outlay. It is necessary to use this changed set of events in making the decision.

Solution 6 – Correct

A correct description of the three events which can occur with an outlay of $400 are:

Income	Utility of Income	Probability	Expectation
$ – 400	– 60	·25	– 15
600	46	·50	23
1,600	56	·25	14
			—
		Expected Utility	22

The decision based on this analysis is to undertake the investment since the expected utility is greater than the utility of $0.

A SINGLE LOTTERY

To help explain why solutions 4 or 5 are not correct, let us consider the simple time 1 lottery and assume that the investor indicates that he is willing to pay $50 to play the gamble once (in this situation there is no subsequent lottery).

The decision-maker is indifferent between \$200 for certain and the lottery (both have utilities of 25).

$$0.5\ U(\$0) + 0.5\ U(\$1,000) = U(\$200)$$
$$0.5 \times 0 + 0.5 \times 50 = 25.$$

Now assume that the question is asked of the decision maker, 'What is the maximum amount you would pay for the lottery?' Assume the answer is \$50. This implies that the utility of the simple lottery with a cost of \$50 would then be zero (i.e. the decision maker would be indifferent as to whether or not the lottery was undertaken). The two outcomes are now:

$$\$-50 \text{ if he loses (\$10 less the cost of \$50)}$$
$$950 \text{ if he wins (\$1,000 less the cost of \$50).}$$

The expected utility of the lottery is:

Income	Utility	Probability	Expectation
−50	−49·8	·5	−24·9
950	49·8	·5	24·9
			$E(U) =$ 0

We could compare the utilities of \$0, \$1,000 and minus \$50.

Dollars	U(\$)	Probability	Expectation
\$0	0	·5	0
1,000	50	·5	25
−50	−49·8	1·0	−49·8
			$E(U) =$ −24·8

Here we have a negative utility measure for the lottery, indicating that the investment is not acceptable. However, the description of the possible events is not correct. There is not a probability of 1 that there will be a loss of \$50 (though there is an outlay of \$50) and the two events \$0 and \$1,000 are impossible if there is a cost of \$50 (the two events − \$50 and \$950 are possible).

It is extremely important that the possible events be

described correctly. If this is done then an outlay of X has a different meaning than a loss of X. It is true that the entire outlay may be a loss, and when the utility of this event is properly weighted by the probability of the event, we have a meaningful measure of value.

It is tempting to compare the $200 certainty equivalent and the $50 outlay and accept the investment since the net difference is a positive $150. This is not correct since it leaves out of consideration the psychological reaction to a possible loss which may result from the investment of $50. The certainty equivalent of $200 is a measure of our reaction to certain possible winnings in the future and leaves out the effect of the initial investment. When this investment outlay is correctly brought into the analysis we adjust the possible events by the amount of the immediate outlay. The two events are then -50 and $950.

Now assume the single lottery has a cost of $200. The two possible events are then:

Income	Utility	Probability	Expectation
$-200	-50	·5	-25
800	48	·5	24
		Expected Utility	-1

The expected utility is negative and we would reject the investment. If we compared the certainty equivalent of $200 and the outlay of $200, we would have concluded that we were indifferent about undertaking the investment.

Another procedure would be to compare the utility of the $200 certainty equivalent with the utility of the outlay. This is the method of Solution 4. With a $200 outlay or a $50 outlay the decision would be to reject, and these are correct decisions based on the utility function which are presented as having been given. However, the correct decisions are just a coincidence.

The procedure is incorrect (though appealing) since it confuses an initial outlay with a loss. This can be seen best by changing the lottery example. Assume the single lottery is now as follows:

Income	Probability
$300	·5
1,200	·5

There is a ·5 probability of winning $300 and a ·5 probability of winning $1,200. Assume it costs $200 to play the lottery. Should we play?

The expected utility of the lottery is 46 and the certainty equivalent is $600.

$$0·5\ U(\$300) + 0·5\ U(\$1,200) = 0·5 \times 40 + 0·5 \times 52 = 46.$$
$$U(\$X) = 46$$
$$X = \$600.$$

The utility of an outlay of $200 is −50, and since this is greater than 46 the investment should be rejected, but this is absurd. The investor cannot lose, with the two possible outcomes $100 and $1,000. The correct answer may be obtained by correctly describing the possible outcomes and computing the expected utility of the lottery.

Net Income	Utility	Probability	Expectation
100	20	·5	10
1,000	50	·5	25
			—
		Expected Utility	35

This analysis clearly shows that the investment is desirable. It will be desirable for any individual who has a utility function for money which is everywhere increasing.

The suggested procedure is to convert sequential lotteries to an equivalent single immediate lottery and then compute the expected utility of the equivalent lottery. If the expected utility is greater than the utility of zero dollars, the lottery is acceptable.

CONCLUSION

We have surveyed several aspects of quantitative decision-making and considered the future of the art, but the reader should not assume that we have completely covered the subject. For example, while we have considered decision-making under uncertainty where time is a factor, we have not systematically considered the interaction of investments and the necessity of considering the entire asset mix when considering a new investment. In the future we can expect decision making to become more quantitative in the sense that more models will be built of decision processes, and more data will be presented to administrators. However, one should not expect to find a world where judgement and emotion are completely removed from the decision process. At their best the quantitative models of the future will incorporate systematically the judgements of the decision-makers so that they may be brought to bear on the decision. Rather than being eliminated, the administrators' insights and experience will be extended in a manner that will more effectively bring his desires and knowledge into the decision process.

Part III

FOUNDATIONS OF THE INVESTMENT DECISION

GEORGE A. TAYLOR

Professor of Engineering and Management,
The Thayer School of Engineering,
Dartmouth College

George A. Taylor served as an executive with General Electric Company and the Ingersoll-Rand Company for twenty years before leaving industry to develop his original ideas on the subject of Decision-Making.

Since joining Dartmouth College he has been the author of three books, *Managerial and Engineering Economy: Economic Decision-Making*, D. Van Nostrand Company, Princeton, New Jersey, 1964; *The Development of Creativity in Europe*, Dartmouth College, 1967; *Managerial and Engineering Decision-Making: The Improvement of Plans and Operations*, a thirty-one chapter book to be published by the McGraw-Hill Book Company.

In addition to his academic work he consults with industry and heads the consulting group, Industrial Development Associates.

Mr Taylor has greatly contributed to the development of executives in over 225 companies who come from afar to take his annual five-day courses in Decision-Making. These courses, as noted in the book, are the accumulation of 25 years' work in preparing the subject so that executives can use it as a powerful tool for competitive leadership. Usually given high in the White Mountains of New Hampshire, the courses have also been given in many other ports of call.

Chapter Ten

THE EXECUTIVE ROLES OF THE BUSINESSMAN

THERE is a problem in business that begins with the new college graduate on his first day in industry and sometimes continues throughout his entire business career. The college graduate, although educated in the newest disciplines and eager to succeed, is very likely to be lost on his first job. Confused about his new role, he has many questions about his new environment and his place in it. How can he participate? What is he expected to do? How can he use his exceptional qualifications for success? What are the other members of the organization up to? Certainly the activities he observes: answering the telephone, running about, working overtime – none of these things that he sees around him can of themselves define the path for success. In fact he may even become disillusioned about the profession which he thought would be inspirational and challenging. But regardless of his initial confusion, many a young man eventually adopts a rather meaningless pattern and gives up on the question, 'What is my role as an executive?'

It is too bad if one's formal education may not answer this question prior to his being thrust into industry. Sometimes it is many years before the executive who eventually succeeds in industry learns the answer. Sometimes, as we have noted, an executive may never learn the answer.

Finding a useful answer to this question, interested the writer for many years. I was looking for a philosophy, not a long list of components of executive qualifications like a knowledge of statistics, public speaking, computer technology, psychology, and so on. To be sure, these were important but they were only the elements of a greater philosophy and of themselves were meaningless. Hopefully I felt that executive activities of seeming intricacy and diversity could be integrated and explained by defining the fundamental roles of the executive

Hopefully I expected that this might show why a successful business man was successful for the things he had done and unsuccessful for the things he had failed to do. Hopefully it might show that a businessman who had never been heard from really had no concept, or a very poor one, of his role as an executive. Hopefully it might show a businessman, who otherwise would never be heard from, how he could pursue success. If such a philosophy did exist, the benefits would be great not only to each executive but to mankind everywhere.

In a search for such a philosophy we will find many that are too narrow on the one hand or too sophisticated on the other. Of course, 'The executive must be a decision-maker!' But correct as this may be, it is too pat and too sophisticated to help us. We must, in the first place, define in simple terms what a decision-maker is.

In this book we offer such a philosophy. We have been using it with businessmen and graduate students with obvious success over the past 15 years. The material presented here is from introductory chapters of the following larger books by the writer: *Managerial and Engineering Economy: Economic Decision-Making*, D. Van Nostrand Company, Princeton, NJ, 1964; *The Development of Creativity in Europe*, Dartmouth College, Hanover, NH, 1967; *Managerial and Engineering Decision-Making: The Improvement of Plans and Operations* to be published by McGraw-Hill Company, New York, NY; and an article, 'What You Should Know About Your Spending-Decisions', *The Financial Executive*, April 1959. The larger texts cover the many principles, techniques, and 'operational phases' into which we have divided the subject. The present work therefore incorporates under one cover the *foundations* of decision-making expressed separately in the other books.

TWO ROLES OF THE EXECUTIVE

We conclude that every executive has only two roles. (Do we imply an easier life for executives? We will try to show it will be better; it could be easier.) The first role of the executive is to maintain the standards that have been established for the operations over which he has responsibility and authority. This role, of course, requires constant vigilance and corrective action because it is a general rule that performance will deteriorate from standard unless continuously supervised and adjusted. This fundamental executive function is aimed at maintaining control of the areas charged to him; it is a kind of police action; it might be called a house-keeping function. And to be sure, in this role the executive may find a full-time job often requiring exceptional time and effort.

The decision-making required in this role consists of recognizing variances from standard and applying corrections. However the degree of decision-making is often not very high because in many cases the corrections have also been standardized. In fact, in modern companies more and more of the process of detection and correction is being transferred to machines. On the other hand in certain decadent companies this role has been so well performed that they are doing things today exactly as they were doing them decades ago – if they are still in business today.

Clearly it cannot be that the only role of the executive is to maintain the status quo. He has a second and most important role: to destroy existing standards and substitute better ones. Whereas the first role maintains operations and holds the status quo, the second changes these.

This role, in which the executive conceives and develops improvements in the areas charged to him, is his creative role.

THE MOST DIFFICULT ROLE

As we will show in later definitions, it is in his second role, his creative role, that the executive must become an important decision-maker. And in this role he must be competent to make decisions with minimum effort, in the least time, on the correct topics, to an adequate level, according to the right criteria, with fewest failures, and with the greatest acceptance. To do this he must possess sufficient knowledge and skill in the techniques of decision-making to meet the level of performance expected of a man in his position.

His responsibility for this role runs concurrently with his responsibility for his maintenance-of-standards role. Consequently the element of time becomes important. He cannot experiment with the *process* of decision-making on every project; he should therefore be educated in it in advance. Furthermore decision-making employs the two highest modes of thinking of which man is capable: creative thinking and judicial thinking.

Whereas, as we mentioned earlier, machines can be used to police some standard operations, creating new standards of performance is a role which only man can perform.

THE PROCESS OF CREATIVE THINKING

As we have indicated the decision-making role of the executive begins with creative thinking. But advice like: work, think, be considerate, be ethical, be effective, be tough, be creative, think creatively, and so on, can be meaningless unless the *process* to be performed can be defined in terms of an entirely operational system. Before we can be content with the phrase 'creative thinking' we must therefore define it.

Let us observe that what the executive actually does when he performs his creative role is to *conceive alternatives* to the existing standards which he has selected to improve. This observation forms the basis of our definition:

'Creative thinking is the generation of alternatives according to accepted criteria.'*

The reader will note that this is an *operational* definition. It specifies that to perform creatively one generates alternatives to existing forms, operations, or concepts. And then he continues to generate alternatives to these alternatives because creative thinking is an iterative process, a continuous striving to conceive the 'best' alternative.

Since we don't have the space to prove this here, we suggest the reader test the previous definition on a project of his own choice such as writing, sculpturing, designing a machine, improving a process, a policy, or even improving a human-relations situation.

This definition also leads inevitably to the thesis that every person can generate alternatives and with competent instruction in the process can learn to do it exceptionally well. Our experience in the past 15 years offers convincing proof of that thesis.

THE PROCESS OF DECISION-MAKING

The previous reasoning will also inevitably lead us to the following operational definition of decision-making:

Decision-making consists of two fundamental components:
  (a) the generation of alternative courses of action and;
  (b) the selection from these of the best course of action.

The reader will observe that decision-making relies on

* A complete explanation for including the phrase 'according to accepted criteria' will not be attempted here; however, a partial one is given in the section titled 'Satisfaction as a Criterion for Decision-Making'.

The points concerned in the definition of objectives and the analysis of the problem have already been discussed by William T. Morris in Part I. This is, of course, a pre-requisite to the generation of alternatives for decision-making.

two fundamental modes of thinking,* first, creative thinking for the generation of alternatives, and second, judicial thinking for the selection of the best alternative. And the reader will recognize that our definition of decision-making disagrees with the usual one found in the literature of the subject that decision-making is (merely) the *discrimination* between courses of action. Should I go to Paris or to Rome? Should I attend the game or see it on television? Should I use this sales distributor or that? Should I buy machine *A* or machine *B*? Decision-making is more than that.

Decision-making is a two-step process because no decision-maker may subsequently avoid his responsibility for a bad decision by proving that he chose the best of two poor courses of action while he failed to create a course of action that a man of his stature should have conceived. A decision-maker's authority is reserved to him instead of his subordinates on the expectation that he will find the winning courses of action wherever they may be. He is expected to go beyond applying modern evaluative and judicial techniques to two poor courses of action. To *find* the best contenders prior to selection employs creative thinking in contrast to and opposed to judicial thinking.

So even if the decision-maker may be presented with a 'complete' list of alternatives by his subordinates, he nevertheless may not excuse himself if it turns out that the best alternative, the one that should have been conceived, was not on the list.

In anticipation of the tests to be applied before adopting a proposal, we must realize that the final test will be whether someone else thinks of a better alternative soon after the decision is adopted. He may be a competitor who conceives a better alternative or he may be a fire fighter called in to put out the blaze resulting from a defective alternative. The only answer to that is to conceive all the alternatives *prior* to choosing the best.

* George A. Taylor – *Managerial and Executive Decision-Making: The Improvement of Plans and Operations*, (McGraw-Hill, NY). Chapter 1.

The reader of course recognizes that generating alternatives is *what* you do in performing the creative process, whereas *how* you generate alternatives with competence forms the basis of a whole course of instruction in the subject.* By instruction in the principles and techniques for generating alternatives the executive can greatly improve his ability as a decision-maker.

ECONOMIC DECISION-MAKING

Economic Decision-Making is a term used to describe the second fundamental of decision-making – the *selection* of the best alternative from among the total array of alternatives that have been conceived. This selection should be made by modern methods employing the criteria which customarily govern man's behavior, that is by correct legal and ethical standards, humanitarian considerations, and competent quantitative tests of profitability.

QUALITATIVE TESTS OF A DECISION

We maintain that the ethical and humanitarian consequences of a decision, not just the materialistic results (like saving labor or materials) must be included in the tests of a decision. We aver that unethical and inhumane courses of action are unprofitable and the 'losses' can never be made to justify the gains. This is not an attempt to put a dollar sign on goodness. We should not interpret this to mean that if we can't see how the losses will exceed the gains one should approve unethical and inhumane actions. We hold this to be an absolute test,† not one of degree as are always the tests of monetary investments.

The previous statements also conform to a basic requisite

* *Ibid.*, Chapters 3–26.
† The absolute effects of ethical aberrations are implied in Matthew 16:26, 'For what is a man profited, if he shall gain the whole world, and lose his own soul?'

in decision-making, *all the consequences must be included in the evaluation*. The businessman must therefore judge, not only by the quantification of the materialistic consequences of his proposal, but by the qualitative and irreducible consequences (i.e. ethical, humanitarian) which he is incapable of reducing to dollars.* Of course, this requires a decision-maker to judge what is ethical and what is humane. We would like very much to speak more about this, but the reader is aware that this, too, is an extensive discipline in itself. However let us conclude with these brief observations. Man has traditionally gone to war, sacrificed his immediate comforts, given his life to defend his principles. The consequences of unethical acts are inexorable and the penalties can be expected to continue long after 'honest' mistakes will be forgotten. Characteristically, proposals which promise to increase immediate profits in violation of ethical or humane criteria fail to present a complete analysis of their consequences; their irreducibles are incomplete. Conversely proposals which will improve the company's humanitarian and ethical relationships with its workers or the public might very well be very profitable even though the reducible (monetary) effects do not so indicate.

SATISFACTION AS A CRITERION FOR DECISION-MAKING

Relevant to our previous discussion we might conclude that 'benefits' or 'satisfaction' provide a more complete interpretation of 'return on the investment' or profits than an exhibit limited to monetary returns. Profit must, in fact, be the total return, reducible and irreducible. Of course, a complete analysis of the irreducibles increases the difficulty of the decision-maker; however the longer we are

* This is rather more difficult than the writer implies since all human benefits have some financial cost and one is regularly called upon to trade-off these social benefits in order to keep within a specified budget; e.g. hospitals against schools, or poor relief against roads. Hence the importance of setting the right philosophical objective before generating alternatives.

associated with the economics of decision-making the more ways we find to quantify many so-called irreducibles.

Since we hold these tests apply to all decisions of mankind, we are often asked how they may apply to creative thinking in the fine arts. These tests are, of course, likely to be irreducible. Thus if a painter proposes a 'theme' the criteria for its adoption is its 'profit' to somebody, that is the degree of satisfaction, pleasure, enjoyment, or benefit that the painting will bring the owner in return for its purchase. So if the painter is interested in a profitable sale of his art he can continue to search for the alternative which brings the greatest satisfaction in the market-place. Of course, a given artist may believe that his type of art will achieve the greatest notice so his iteration of alternatives aims to maximize his own satisfaction. But where self-satisfaction may be the criteria for selection we note that it (satisfaction) is the return on the investment of effort or money needed to produce the creation.

Perhaps the reader may now understand why we included the term 'according to accepted criteria' in the definition of creative thinking. One who has studied the creative process knows the principal rule that one's imagination must be uninhibited. We believe these criteria, though they may be called 'constraints', do not deter creativity. In fact these are the guides for creative action. They must be regarded from a positive viewpoint: we are searching for more efficient, more ethical, more humane courses of action. By these guides we can conduct a more efficient excursion. Nevertheless we must shrewdly beware of constraints in the imaginative phase of the decision-making process. We can, for example, show how a set of 'objectives' may become a barrier to good decision-making.

EXECUTIVES CAN IMPROVE THEIR CREATIVE DECISION-MAKING ABILITIES

The first step in decision-making, to create all the potential courses of action that the situation demands, is a great challenge for every decision-maker. We have made this step operational by pointing out that whether the innovator is creating an improved policy, product, machine, production process, management system, pattern for human relations, or even an artistic creation, he engages in generating a continuum of alternatives to all the elements of the 'project' that he has selected and then synthesizes the part into a feasible whole.

While this procedure *is* operational, the decision-maker may still have much to learn about how to operate it, that is *how* to generate alternatives. Even without any education in the process he can generate alternatives because his imagination enables him to conceive alternatives to things that he perceives. But when he encounters the complex problems within his sphere of business he cannot rely on an untrained ability to generate the needed alternatives. To qualify as a professional manager or administrator he must conceive the highest quality of alternatives in a competitive environment; his serious competitors may even include those who work in his own company. Most often he must do this within a time limit while conducting his other responsibilities. He must do this without expending himself in the enormous process of creation, but he may not offer a poor proposal either. His ideas must equal the quality which would be expected of a man of his stature. His suggestions must encompass all the reasonable alternatives at that level. For example, he should not propose a mechanical device while overlooking an electrical or chemical device that would do the job better; nor should he propose a procedure while overlooking the policy which would make the procedure unnecessary. He should be adept in identifying and performing the 'phases' of the creative process because to overlook one or to perform it badly is to invite misfortune.*

The first essential element of the decision-making process, generation of alternatives, and the second essential, selec-

* *op. cit.*, divides the creative process into the 'phases' in which the decision-maker engages. Chapters 3–11.

tion of the best alternatives, are separate disciplines. Both are large areas of learning and both are teachable. Fifteen years ago the writer began teaching these disciplines in special programs for executives and our experience certainly gives satisfactory evidence of this. The encouragement we can offer to every manager and prospective manager is that since the procedures of decision-making are operational each can greatly increase his inherent abilities to perform these modes of thinking by a competent course of instruction.

Nevertheless both of these disciplines, as the reader suspects, are the most difficult in which to acquire executive competence. In the first place they employ man's highest modes of thinking. Secondly, they probably were not taught to the executive in college. Thirdly, they are very extensive bodies of knowledge. Consequently we do find that executives need and benefit from personalized instruction in these disciplines of decision-making.

Now let us identify the philosophies and the basic principles that are the foundations for the *selection* of the best courses of action giving particular attention to the economic (or profit) criteria. These criteria often lend themselves to quantitative methods as we shall see.

QUANTITATIVE TESTS OF A DECISION

Profitability is sometimes criticized as materialistic but it is also responsible for man's incentive, morale, achievement, deferment of desires, and so on, as many economic texts have illustrated. Through profitable enterprises, in the sense we have defined profitability, we can relieve man's suffering, satisfy his basic needs, increase his standard of living, and provide him with leisure time which he can use to improve himself and his environment, including its ethical and humanitarian constituents.

We propose to extend our discussion to quantitative examples because these quantitative tests provide a more direct insight into the principles for selecting alternatives.

They also provide a clear communication to the businessman which he may not overlook in his total consideration of a decision. The quantitative area of decision-making is therefore also discussed extensively in the literature on the subject – and, necessarily from a mathematical point of view.

Recent magazine articles have been encouraging the businessman to apply mathematics to his management decisions. Obviously, this is the method of scientific management: the use of mathematical tools whenever a problem can be quantified. For example, the scientific approach to the problem of whether to spend money to install either a semi-automatic or a fully-automatic manufacturing process is to make a mathematical analysis of the profitability of deciding for one or the other. Management will have a more accurate guide to this decision if it can be shown that the fully-automatic process pays, for example, a 30% rate of return on it relative to the semi-automatic. Undoubtedly, the businessman has always wished to show this kind of mathematical proof of his decisions but finds himself uninformed and untutored in such analyses of his spending decisions.

With mathematics and science growing profusely, the businessman finds that every expert in expenditure evaluations apparently suggests a different method. Take, for example, the methods suggested for the analysis of equipment replacement: every method has a different name, employs a different formula, and even seems to be based on completely different theory and fundamental principles although each is intended for the same purpose.* These various methods require considerable time for study and digestion even by the expert in the subject so what of the businessman who has neither the time nor the background? Our objective here is to provide the businessman with the fundamentals of his spending decisions and to give him an understanding of the principles on which the mathematical analysis is based.

* e.g. annual cost, present value (DCF), rate of return (yield).

Chapter Eleven

MAKING INVESTMENT DECISIONS

TWO TYPES OF SPENDING DECISIONS

BASICALLY there are only two types of spending decisions. The first type concerns long-lived or fixed assets like machinery and equipment that will give long company service. Its common characteristics are that it involves future spending commitments as well as present and the equipment items are all depreciable. The second type concerns expenditures which are entirely in the present and carry no commitments for future expenditures.

Our discussion will focus on spending decisions of the first type because these are among the poorest of all management decisions. These are the decisions that have been under fire in management magazines and conferences. Fortunately they are decisions that can be corrected with qualified training in the use of a proper technique.

In general, executives handle the second type of spending decision more competently because it can be solved by mathematics well within their grasp. Few management decisions are of this type, however, so we will not consider them here. Nevertheless some have important influences on profits and may even require complex mathematics. Examples of such problems are: make or buy; dividing loads between machines or departments; increment costs; economic lot sizes; and so on.

SPENDING DECISIONS AS INVESTMENTS

Prerequisite to the analysis of spending decisions is the understanding that all are investments. Contrary to the concept of 'spending' which the name suggests, spending decisions are actually investments on which rates of profit can be computed. This employs the term 'investment' precisely, not as a figure of speech. The following examples, admittedly simplified, illustrate this fact about spending decisions.*

First Example: ANALYSIS OF A SPENDING DECISION FOR MECHANIZING A PROCESS. A company proposes to mechanize an existing process by installing a machine costing $10,000. The resulting annual operating disbursements for such items as labor, fuel, taxes, repairs, and maintenance are estimated to be $5,000. The machine will be required on this service for 10 years with prospective zero salvage value at that date. This machine is proposed to replace a manual process costing $8,000 a year for labor.

How can this expenditure be treated as an investment?

Answer: If $10,000 is spent now for a machine, only $5,000 a year, instead of $8,000 a year, must be disbursed for the next 10 years. Lower disbursements of $3,000 a year mean that the corporation's net income after disbursements will be higher by that amount. However, this $3,000 increase in income is acquired only by spending $10,000 for a new machine. The investment viewpoint is simply this: Is it profitable to invest $10,000 now in order to receive $3,000 a year for 10 years?

We will show later how the businessman can compute the profitability of this investment.

---

* The examples of this chapter are engineering-orientated. It is relatively simple, however, for the interested reader to think of similar examples of spending decisions in other management activities, such as marketing and manpower. Examples of investment problems in other areas of business are given in the literature cited in this Part. See also A. J. Merrett and Allen Sykes, *The Finance and Analysis of Capital Projects*, (Longmans, 1963); H. Bierman and S. Smidt, *The Capital Budgeting Decision*, (Collier-Macmillan, rev. ed. 1966); A. J. Merrett and Allen Sykes, *Capital Budgeting and Company Finance* (Longmans, 1966).

Second Example: ANALYSIS OF A SPENDING DECISION
TO REPLACE AND MODERNIZE A PROCESS. A company proposes to replace an existing machine with the
latest automatic model costing $10,000. Annual operating
disbursements for the proposed machine are predicted to
be $5,000 and its life on this service is expected to be
10 years with zero salvage at that date. The present
machine can be sold for $2,000 in the open market;
in 10 years its salvage value is expected to be zero; and
its annual operating disbursements on this service are
$7,000.

How can this expenditure be treated as an investment?

Answer: The investment viewpoint is this: By investing an
additional $8,000 today, disbursements can be reduced by
$2,000 a year for the next 10 years. The question is whether
to increase the level of investment from $2,000 to $10,000 –
that is, whether to invest an additional $8,000. Therefore,
should the firm invest $8,000 to get $2,000 a year for 10
years?

This investment, too, can be analysed by investment
mathematics as can be shown later.

Third Example: ANALYSIS OF A SPENDING DECISION
TO DETERMINE WHICH MACHINE TO INSTALL. A
company will require a machine to perform a certain
process. A semi-automatic machine can be purchased for
$5,000, and its annual operating disbursements will be
$6,000. Alternatively a fully automatic machine can be
purchased for $9,000 and its annual operating disburse-
ments will be $4,000. The life of either machine on this
service is expected to be 10 years.

How can this expenditure be treated as an investment?

Answer: The investment problem is whether to invest
an additional $4,000 in order to receive $2,000 a year for
10 years. The only question is: Should the level of investment be increased from $5,000 to $9,000? The argument for
increasing it is the additional annual income of $2,000 for
10 years.

Even though neither of the machines is presently owned, the question is identical to that in Example Two: Should the extra investment be made?

The reader should note that, regardless of the choice at least $5,000 must be spent because, as stated, the company 'will require a machine to perform a certain process'. Example Three presumes that a prior investment analysis has determined the profitability of requiring at least the $5,000 machine for the process. The following example illustrates this point.

Fourth Example: ANALYSIS OF A SPENDING DECISION TO DETERMINE WHETHER TO EXPAND THE BUSINESS. If a certain machine is purchased for $5,000 its entire output can be sold for $10,000 every year. The total annual cost of producing the product including the operation of the machine and selling the product is $7,000 a year. The machine is expected to provide this service for 10 years.

How would this problem be set up as an investment? Answer: The question is whether $5,000 should be invested in order to receive an annual net income, after disbursements, of $3,000 a year for 10 years.

Every businessman recognizes the investment concept in the last example but too many fail to see the investment concept in the first three examples of spending decisions. What they do not seem to realize is that all decisions are investments.

These four examples are intended to illustrate *all* the business decisions of the type we are examining. The first illustrates a proposal to mechanize, the second to modernize, the third to increase mechanization and machine efficiency, the fourth to engage in a new or expanded enterprise. In the broadest sense all are tests of replacement, that is whether to continue a present course of action (or a present *concept* as in the Third Example) with another one. This idea will be developed further in the following section.

THE DECISION IS ALWAYS BETWEEN ALTERNATIVES

One obstacle to the use of the investment concept in industry is the failure to see the proposal as an alternative to an incumbent investment. However, we will note in each of the examples in the last section that the investment depends on the existence of an alternative course of action. A bit of reflection should convince us that there can never be less than two alternatives. At the very minimum the decision reduces to, 'Should I continue what I am doing now or should I make the proposed expenditure?' Even if it seems reasonable to define what you are doing as doing nothing, it is not hard to discover that doing nothing is a real alternative in an economic sense. Doing nothing can be very uneconomical; for instance, leaving money in a strong box instead of investing it can be a very expensive way of doing nothing.

Doing nothing is a course of action which represents maintenance of the status quo – like keeping the same policies, the same products, the same designs, the same methods of production.

Too often in industry the capital budget is presented and considered for approval without any mention of the alternatives to the proposed expenditures. Management should, at least, insist on knowing the alternative (and its cost pattern) that the proposed expenditure will replace. Management should in addition insist on knowing what other alternatives were considered beyond the proposed one.

THE CRITERIA FOR APPROVING SPENDING DECISIONS

Because all decisions are investments, the basic criteria for approving them should be familiar to us. Not so familiar, however, will be the criteria for selecting only those investments that contribute to the profit maximization of the entire firm. These criteria are:

1. The invested money must be recovered.
2. An acceptable rate of return must be paid on the investment.
3. The acceptable rate of return must be higher than the firm's capital use-rate.
4. The acceptable rate of return must also be higher than the firm's cutoff rate.

All of these criteria can be established by mathematical analysis. In addition to these criteria the security of the investment can be estimated by determining a probable factor of safety. At this point we should mention that these analyses can be performed by mathematics well within the grasp of the average business executive.

IMPORTANCE OF THE COST OF CAPITAL

The obligation to pay for the capital it uses binds the business to its suppliers of funds. Debt capital binds the company to the lenders with all the force of common and statutory law so that failure to pay interest or principal can mean a complete loss of equity. Plowback capital binds the company to its shareholders and failure to pay satisfactory dividends becomes cause for removal of the management through the vote of the shareholders. It is important, therefore, that the management judge every spending decision in the light of the ability of that investment to meet the obligations to the suppliers of debt and equity capital.

Every management decision creates a cost, every decision involves an alternative, and every decision can be evaluated as an investment. Every manager should treat every decision as an investment with the knowledge that the rate of return on the investment must at least meet the cost of the firm's capital. Obviously, this way of thinking provides the guide to all management action and is an absolutely indispensable test of correct management action. It is therefore amazing how few executives have had adequate training in the evaluation of capital expenditures. It is also very gratifying to see how it changes a manager's entire way of thinking once he understands the procedure and learns to use it as a tool. This way of thinking, often described as 'economic awareness', invariably becomes the major identification of successful business leaders.

IMPORTANCE OF THE CUTOFF RATE

If the demand for funds exceeds the supply, a company will not be meeting its profit potential if it invests at a return which will recover only its cost of capital. The firm will not be maximizing the earnings on its investments until it governs its expenditure by a cutoff rate.

The economic need for a cutoff arises when the demand for funds for capital expenditures exceeds the supply in order to ensure that the available funds will be allocated only to the investments that promise the best rates of return. Whenever money is allocated to a project promising a rate of return below the cutoff rate, a better investment at a higher rate of return will be denied. Good management recognizes that it is not enough to meet the rates of return established by the obligations on debt and equity but every dollar must be invested at its highest possible rate of return.

The cutoff rate is the theoretical rate of return of the poorest investment opportunity which will be financed by the last dollar available from the firm's supply for capital investment.* It recognizes that not enough money exists to saturate all the good investments down through the cost of capital.

In general, we expect that the demands will exceed the supply of funds. In any company where the demands do not exceed the supply, the situation is prima-facie evidence that

---

* i.e. the marginal economic rate under the prevalent business conditions of risk, future prospects, corporate long-term strategy, etc. Note that this means capital availability *only* up to the level at which management desires to create such a financial structure of the firm. It does not mean borrowing investment capital up to the last penny that *could* be borrowed.

the management is failing in its obligations to find profitable investments within the firm; failing to suggest better methods, processes, and equipment; failing to replace old and obsolete equipment; in short, failing to be creative. It is management's duty to suggest expenditures, not to avoid them.

It is also management's duty to supply the funds necessary to finance the good investments that are available. When the amount of plowback capital is more or less fixed, as it usually is, management faces the problem of whether to increase the supply by adding to the firm's funded debt or by adding to its equity capital.

The forces that generate the supply of funds also bring the cutoff rate closer to the cost of capital. On the other hand, the drive of management that causes the demand to exceed the supply brings the cutoff rate farther from the cost of capital. It is clearly the duty of all management to increase these demands by a never-ending search for better investments, and it is the duty of financial management to supply the capital for these demands subject to the restrictions arising from debt limits, loss of control by granting new equity, and so on.

EVALUATING THE SPENDING DECISIONS

What is the mathematical model for computing the rate of return on the investment represented by the spending decisions? The problem is to compute the annual rate of return on the investment recognizing that the investment must be fully recovered. We can give a sample illustration using the data in Example One. In that example an investment of $10,000 was predicted to save $3,000 a year for 10 years. The measure of the investment will be a uniform annual rate of return computed after the recovery of capital. Computing the rate of return has the advantage, compared to annual-cost and present-worth methods,* of permitting

* Briefly; whereas the rate of return is expressed as a percentage, the annual cost is the predicted constant cost for each year during the

comparisons of proposals in different departments or divisions of the business (i.e., a 50% rate of return is more attractive than 30%) and permitting the demands to be laddered for capital-budgeting purposes.

The mathematical model based on the logarithmic or exponential growth of investment mathematics will contain binomials to the nth power (tenth, in this case), but by the use of specially prepared tables* the solution for the rate of return can be obtained by algebra. The simple model and solution for Example One will be:

10,000 X (capital recovery factor) = 3,000
so,　　(crf) = 3,000/10,000 = 0·3
and from tables for (crf) for 10 years:
Rate of Return on the Investment = 27·3%.

The factor for the recovery of capital, (crf), is one of a number of such factors available to the analyst for solving these problems. These factors may be expressed as discrete or continuous functions. For example the discrete function used in the above equation is:

$$\frac{i\,(1+i)^{10}}{(1+i)^{10} - 1} = 0\cdot3$$

and the solution for the unknown rate i is 27·3%. By the use of tables giving these factors for many values of i and n (years), laborious solution of the equations like the above is avoided. Furthermore by the use of electronic computers the analyst can get solutions from the most complex decision situations in a matter of seconds. However as most decisions are more complex than the simple illustration given here, education is necessary to set up models of the alternatives which the executive conceives.

---

life of the proposal; while the present worth is the sum of all the costs through the life of the proposal expressed in terms of today's monetary values.

* George A. Taylor, *Managerial and Engineering Economy: Economic Decision-Making*, D. Van Nostrand Company, Princeton, NJ, 1964, Appendix.

The reader is warned that the subject can be oversimplified if it is limited to information gleaned from a magazine article or a handbook, and can be overcomplicated if it plainly disregards the fact that the subject must be handled by businessmen and not mathematicians. A training program is also dangerously oversimplified if it merely gives the businessman cookbook formulas for the solution of every kind of spending decision. As engineers learned years ago, handbook engineering unsupported by basic knowledge can have serious repercussions.

OTHER FACTORS IN THE INVESTMENT ANALYSIS

Actually an understanding of the mathematics is the least of the knowledge required for the analysis of spending decisions. The analyst must understand the factors of obsolescence, deterioration, economic life, corporate income tax, salvage value, hazards and risks, factors of safety, changes in dollar purchasing power, treatment of irreducibles, strategic investments, and a knowledge of the capital use-rate and the cutoff rate.

As an example, let us show how one of these, the factor of economic life, is important in a spending decision analysis. In most situations, the predicted savings will not last over the entire accounting life or useful life of the proposed equipment. These predicted savings exist only for the duration of the service for which you are proposing to acquire the equipment. In the *useful* life period of most equipment, a primary service life is followed by successive periods of degraded service. Therefore when proposing the acquisition of a new equipment, the predictions, including the prediction of economic life, are circumscribed by the primary or initial life period. It is generally beyond anyone's ability to predict what the *subsequent* degraded services will be, no less the utilization, annual savings, and length of life in each of these services. The prediction of this initial economic life period depends on a knowledge of how the class of equipment under consideration conforms to various conceivable patterns of obsolescence and deterioration.

The mathematical model must therefore reflect all these elements of this one factor, economic life. But it must correctly express all the other factors, too, from income tax to the uncertainty of predictions.*

* The problems of scrap value, economic life, uncertainty, and sensitivity of estimates are all discussed in the previously cited works of George Taylor, Hal Bierman and Sy Smidt, A. J. Merrett and Allen Sykes.

Chapter Twelve

EVALUATION METHODS EVALUATED

COMMENTS ON SOME POPULAR METHODS

SINCE industry uses various methods of analysing spending decisions, let us briefly review the systems in general use today. My experience as a result of assigning 30 to 40 men a year over a four-year period to investigate industries' procedures for the analysis of spending decisions failed to reveal one company, in the 120 to 160 companies visited, that employed a mathematical investment concept of a spending decision. A few companies were found that used an annual-cost concept but too frequently these annual costs were computed incorrectly through the blind and faulty use of formulas. The alternative methods used by industry which this research uncovered are briefly reported here.

The method which we decided to call the *squeaky wheel technique* judges the need for a favorable decision to spend money on the volume of noise accompanying the appropriations request. It is based upon the principle that 'the squeaky wheel gets the grease'. It is not a technique for the approval of all spending requests but where it is applied it works. It works simply because management has no way of refusing the request. If management could compute the rate of return on this spending decision to show that it is, for example, only an inadequate 1% before taxes, it would be rejected, but management cannot compute it because the prerequisite for this method is that no bona-fide method of evaluation exists in the company.

The method we called the *intuitive technique* hardly needs description. It is the substitution of management hunches for mathematical analysis. The inherent danger in hunch decisions is that they seemingly do not necessitate collecting any quantitative facts, no less the exact and complete facts. However no degree of common sense can make up for the absence of facts or the presence of incorrect facts. It seems an easy method but it isn't, because every incorrect decision must re-emerge for a new solution. It is very likely the basis for an endless chain of effort – and losses.

A method which we called the *necessity technique* has the most insidious possibilities. The necessity method seems to eliminate all need for mathematical analyses of spending decisions. A new machine is approved only when it becomes obvious that the existing one can no longer perform its job. This, of course, saves wear and tear on the analyst and ridicules the need of mathematical procedures to determine what any person can see without glasses: replacement is absolutely necessary because the machine is beyond repair.

The necessity method is one of the most expensive malpractices that industry could use. Its adoption automatically puts that company on a downward path. It provides a successful policy for minimizing profits because it protects high operating costs. If the firm's competitors are meanwhile maximizing their profits through cost-reduction and income-expansion opportunities, there will come a day when they can promote a reduction in the price of goods that will squeeze the high-cost company out of the market. In New England we have seen industries descend over this path. Nevertheless, not long ago a top financial executive in a large New York firm told me, 'We know when to replace a machine and we don't need to compute it. No mathematical analysis is necessary to tell us when a machine won't run anymore'.

This philosophy can govern a company, a community, or even a nation. George Terborgh, Director of Research of Machinery and Allied Products Institute, has much to say about the ill-effects of a policy 'to scrap a machine only when it could no longer do the job for which it was originally designed'. His comments were directed toward economic problems in Great Britain but the effects are the same wherever the necessity policy prevails.*

To understand the economic losses associated with the necessity method let us compute the cost of a failure to replace when replacement was economically due. As we have seen by this method any thought of replacing a machine is rejected if it is still able to perform the duty for which it was purchased. No other reason is sought even though the machine might be 30 to 40 years old. But by completely disregarding the economic reasons for replacement it is almost certain that replacement is long overdue. It is very probable that an economic analysis made when the equipment was 10 to 15 years old would have approved a decision to replace this machine with an improved one. If by the necessity method replacement actually occurs when the machine is 40 years old, the company has been paying extra costs and rejecting extra profits for 25 to 30 years. Furthermore, during this period these profits if reinvested annually at the company's cutoff rate would compound into a great increase in the firm's assets.

To demonstrate this quantitatively let us assume in the foregoing example that an economic test made when the machine was 15 years old would have signalled replacement by a machine having an extra cost of $10,000 and a 15-year economic life based on a 20% capital cutoff rate. It can be shown mathematically that, for this to be so, the annual savings from this machine would have had to be $2,140 a year after income tax. If these annual savings had been retained in the firm they would have produced an annual flow-back or cash-flow of $2,140. Reinvesting this cash-flow at the firm's cutoff rate of 20% would have resulted in a present-day sum of almost $1,010,000 or a net increase in the original $10,000 addition to assets of about $1 million.

The necessity method is of course, very simple. With

* George Terborgh, *Dynamic Equipment Policy* (McGraw-Hill, 1949) page 8. The truth is well evidenced by the poor competitiveness of Britain against Sweden, Germany, Japan and America; the chronic balance of payments crises and threats of devaluation.

it one doesn't have to make decisions. It also has universal applications. Wait until the roof leaks, the business fails, the people revolt, or the war starts. In many of these situations the decision-maker who refused to decide when he had the authority, may no longer have that authority: the company may be out of business, he may be deposed, he may be unable to acquire the forces or the money required to control the disaster which can follow on the wake of his inactivity. In such instances it may be too late to make a satisfactory solution.

The necessity method is one of the examples of the high cost of ignorance in this subject. Furthermore it sometimes takes more than a simple understanding of the subject to detect *corollaries* of the necessity method. For example, consider the situation of a manager who intentionally delays replacement of a machine long after its economic life but proposes replacement prior to the moment of necessity. A delayed replacement always shows a much higher rate of return than a timely one! Will top management judge the value of his suggestion by its high rate of return and reward him accordingly? The reason for the high rate of return is simple: a new machine shows much greater savings in operating disbursements in comparison to a 35-year-old machine than to a 15-year-old machine. It therefore appears to be a better proposal, and it is, but the executive who proposes replacing a 35-year-old machine should not be commended until we know why he didn't propose replacing it 5, 10, 15, 20, or even 25 years ago! Is he in any way responsible for continuing the economic drain on the company's profitability by not replacing the machine when it should have been? If he is, then he should be censured for the delay, not commended for the high rate of return on his present proposal.

Extension of the necessity method beyond the previous illustrations brings us to the brink-of-disaster method. If failure to make a decision at the time when the decision should be made brings on an emergency, should the man who guides us out of the consequences which he brought about claim the recognition and rewards accorded a savior? He is now the decision-maker who must make decisions under the most adverse situations! However if he has purposely delayed in order to bring about an emergency from which he proposes to rescue his people he should be censured or the people should be censured if the delay was caused by their refusal to heed his timely proposal.

A CLOSE LOOK AT THE PAYOUT METHOD

We can readily show that the payout (or payoff) method, although it is a mathematical technique and greatly used in industry, is not an analysis of an investment. The payout period is the time that must elapse before the investment is recovered; as usually computed it is the extra investment divided by the annual savings in disbursements. The payout method, therefore, locates the break-even point between outgo and income. But the computation of a break-even point does not prove the existence of a profitable investment as the following six examples will show.

In these examples each requires an extra investment of $1,000 and promises annual savings of $250. Therefore by the payout method each has a four-year payout period, and if the company policy had established four years or better as the criterion then all six investments will be approved without further analysis.

However, by the proper analysis of these spending decisions we would arrive at much different conclusions. The first step in analysing these as investments is to investigate and predict the economic lives of each. Suppose these are judged to be 3, 4, 5, 6, 8, and 12 years respectively for the six investments. The mathematics will show the respective percent profit earned on each after the recovery of capital to be: minus, zero, 8%, 13%, 19%, and 23%. The 'minus' shows that in the first 'investment' no profit will be earned as, in fact, the capital is not even recovered. The 'zero' indicates that the capital is recovered but no profit is earned. The last four of these proposals earn profits but prior to adoption or rejection these must be compared with the firm's cost of capital and its cutoff rate. Let us assume these are 15% and 20% respectively. Disregarding irreducible factors, our simplified analysis of these six spending decisions suggests that we should approve only one, the one that promises 23%.

Now let us use the break-even point analysis for its proper purpose – to test the security of the investment. All these investments have a computed payout, payoff, payback, or break-even period of four years at zero rate of return. If we compare this with their predicted economic lives, we can observe a factor or margin of safety for each investment. In the first example, the factor of safety is negative because the economic life is three years and the period required for break-even is four; in the second there is no margin for error because the economic life is four years and the period required for break-even is also four. The greatest factor of safety is in the last investment where the predicted economic life of 12 years can be in error by as much as eight years prior to break-even.*

The use of the payout period as the sole test of a spending decision neglects the following fundamental principles:

1. The purpose of an investment is not merely to recover the investment but to make a profit on it.
2. The break-even point of an investment is not a test of its profitability.
3. The payout period of a project is not a test of its security. The test occurs when it is compared to the predicted economic life.
4. Tests of security or sensitivity should be applied to all elements of the predicted investment, not merely to its predicted life.

The payout method therefore results in the following errors:

* *Managerial and Engineering Economy*, 1964, George A. Taylor, pp. 345–6 discusses the elements of a break-even test such as the cost of capital.

1. The payout method gives approval to unacceptable investments having short economic lives.
2. It rejects acceptable investments having long economic lives.
3. The payout method confuses testing the profitability of an investment with its true function: it is a tool of financing to determine the date when the capital will be paid back.

The following illustration completely summarizes the payout method: if a lender were to say, 'I will lend you $1,000 if you will repay it in not more than four years' he would be using the payout method. He would know when he would recover his money. If his only reason for lending money is to get it back by a specified date without regard to earnings then the payout method is the correct one for him.*

* This ignores, of course, the opportunity loss which he sustains by foregoing the profit he could have made by alternative methods of investment such as putting his money in a bank.

Chapter Thirteen

WHY SCIENCE? THE FINAL REASONS AND RESPONSIBILITIES

TWO ESSENTIAL REASONS FOR SCIENTIFICALLY ANALYSING SPENDING DECISIONS

THE magnitude of the firm's spending decisions is sufficient reason for giving time and effort to their analysis. To appreciate this let us see how these decisions are reflected, both in magnitude and quality, in the firm's financial statements.

Beginning with the balance sheet, we note that the expenditures represented by the fixed assets account, which in some companies can amount to nearly three-fourths of the net worth, are all the direct result of previous spending decisions. Furthermore, since the year-by-year sources of funds for these spending decisions are largely from the earned capital, the depreciation reserve, and the funded-debt accounts, the amounts of these accounts also reflect the magnitude of these decisions.

The profit and loss statement, also, reflects both the magnitude and the quality of the firm's spending decisions. All the costs, the disbursements for labor, materials, power – even the expenses for depreciation – are the results of prior investment decisions which would determine today's costs. Similarly, the gross income is basically the result of a spending decision made years ago to engage in this enterprise and to produce this product. The profit and loss statement reflects the company's previous long-term spending decisions which established the standard incomes and the standard costs for a long time to come. Unless new spending decisions are made, the most that efficient management can do is to vary the incomes and costs around the norm established by these standards. The mere fact that the present profit and loss statement and the balance sheet are the image of all these decisions should be sufficient reason for adopting the most scientific approach possible.

The second major reason for adopting a scientific approach is that there is no place to hide from spending decisions. It is often implied by a manager's action that he hopes to escape the responsibility by just not making a decision to spend money. But the question is, 'Can an executive hide from these decisions by refusing to make expenditures?' Obviously, refusing to spend the money is a decision, and the mere fact that one is not aware of the consequences does not mean that he can escape them. For example, if an opportunity exists to spend $10,000 for a new machine that will result in annual savings of $2,500 for 12 years, no one is forced to spend the $10,000. But if he doesn't spend the $10,000 he *must* spend the $2,500 a year in extra disbursements. A decision not to spend money is therefore a decision to continue to pay for the operation of the present machine no matter how uneconomical. In the present example, deciding not to buy the new machine is a positive decision to spend $2,500 a year for 12 years instead of $10,000. Whoever thought he could hide from the decision to spend $10,000 will spend it and more in the long run.

This has given rise to the statement, 'The man who needs a new machine is already paying for it'. We might add that he will pay for the machine without obtaining it. The consequences of avoiding decisions by refusing to spend money is a rejection of savings, a rejection of the most economic equipment, a rejection of the best investments. It results in the gradual narrowing of profits relative to competition, and, if continued, degradation of the operating plant to the point where it becomes too deteriorated and too obsolete to continue in business. The fact is there is no place to hide from spending decisions.

RESPONSIBILITY FOR THE ANALYSIS
OF SPENDING DECISIONS

Every decision-maker, and therefore every manager in the company, should be competent to evaluate and discriminate between the alternatives which he must create in his role as a manager. From our previous definition, this activity is one of the fundamental components of the decision-making process. It is a mode of thinking which each manager must perform for himself as a decision-maker. We noted, too, that this is not solely the process of discriminating between alternatives after generating them; it is the *guide* to executive action *during* the creative process. It provides the innovator with direction to his creative activities and gives the innovator many advantages over one who creates without a sense of objectives. Therefore he cannot delegate this activity.

As we have pointed out, few executives have acquired a competent understanding and ability to use this modern tool of management. Except for a few managers recently out of college, this subject has not been available in executives' formal education. However present executives can (and should) acquire this competence as an essential part of their managerial responsibility. Our experience in conducting executive programs shows that exceptional progress can be made even in only one week of intensive instruction in the subject.

In addition to individual executive competence and responsibility in the subject, the company should maintain a staff responsible for its capital-budgeting activity. This group, out of its superior knowledge of the subject, should set up the standard systems and procedures for managers to follow in computing the rate of return on the investment and in presenting capital-expenditure proposals for approval. It should enumerate the kind of data the company expects to receive and the supporting evidence for it. It should provide not only for a post-audit of decisions but for an audit prior to approval.*

* Although Professor Taylor does not emphasize the point, it has

This staff should also be responsible for communicating its established methods and procedures to all decision-makers; including if necessary, the publication of a company manual with explanatory information. It should provide instruction for executives who are new to the system. The company must realize that among the other advantages of the subject it can also establish a bridge of understanding between executives in finance and those in engineering, planning, production, and marketing.

Most often this staff will be under the direction of the comptroller of the company because he may be responsible under the board of directors for capital budgeting and for allocating funds to the best proposals. In many instances he also takes overall responsibility for promoting projects for improvement of the firm, a dual responsibility which conforms to our definition of decision-making. The comptroller's function will, of course, be amplified by competent decision-making by all members of the firm.

CONCLUSION

In conclusion we hold out great hope to every manager who is on his way to greater responsibilities as a decision-maker. The first reason is he has innate ability in the two modes of thinking used in decision-making. Second, he has had some experience in practising the subject so instruction can be patterned on his experience. Third, it can be shown what phases of the subject he has been performing correctly in his successful ventures and what phases he may have

---

been the editor's experience that however unsatisfactory a method of capital investment is used, companies do make pre-investment studies. It is extremely rare however to find companies monitoring and following up investment decisions after the event and this is an area which offers tremendous potential for the validation of the original decision and decision-making process. Even where a company does use acceptable investment techniques it still needs to follow-up the decisions to see whether the estimates and assumptions made at the time of the investment proposal prove right. In the long run it will also show up those staff whose estimating is unreliable.

omitted or neglected in his less successful ones. Fourth, by learning the organized principles and systematic approach to decision-making, he can perform it more efficiently, reliably, and competitively.

Part IV

THE STOCK DECISION

DR R. A. CUNINGHAME-GREEN

Head of Management Services
Sheffield Regional Hospital Board

Ray A. Cuninghame-Green obtained his Mathematics degree at Oxford and his PhD at Leicester. He has had wide experience as a lecturer on logic, mathematics, computers and operational research and his easy, entertaining style is much loved by his audiences. He has presented a number of full-length television lectures.

In his professional life Dr Cuninghame-Green has divided his time between the computer manufacturing industry and operational research, having been successively employed by Decca Radar, United Steel Companies, Leo Computers, and Cerebos. His current work at the Sheffield Regional Hospital Board carries responsibility for work study, O & M, computer applications and operational research.

He has published articles on logic, mathematics, operational research and is currently writing an introductory textbook on computers. His breadth of practical knowledge and philosophical understanding makes him an excellent Editor of the *Operational Research Quarterly*. He is a member of the Council of the Operational Research Society.

Chapter Fourteen

ONCE UPON A TIME

SUPPOSE that, in preparation for some unique event of national importance – say a coronation – a book publisher produces an expensive high-quality book commemorating the event. He offers it, say, to a bookseller at a wholesale non-returnable price of £3, subject to the bookseller offering it for resale at £5. The bookseller must now make a decision – how large a stock of the book should he purchase? He may calculate that it is very unlikely that he could sell as many as ten copies. But this still leaves a considerable problem. If he buys nine, and finds he sells only three, he will take a loss of £12; if he buys three and finds he could have sold nine, he will have missed the opportunity to make a further £12 profit.

This dilemma has the characteristics of the typical decision problem described in Part II by Hal Bierman:

(i) There are a number of possible actions available to the bookseller. He may buy zero, one, two, ..., up to nine books. It is important, in this connexion, that he cannot obtain further supplies. It would greatly simplify the problem if he could wait to see what demand occurred, and then place his order: and such a possibility would materially change the problem, as we shall discuss later.

(ii) There are a number of possible 'states of nature' which can occur. Demand may come for zero, one, two, ..., up to nine books. Again, it is important, in this connexion, that the selling opportunity is transitory. It would greatly simplify the problem if the demand for coronation souvenirs recurred day after day, and such a possibility would again materially change the problem, as we shall discuss later.

(iii) For each action and each state of nature there is a consequence. The table in Figure 1(a) illustrates, for example, the profit or loss accruing to the bookseller

		STATES OF NATURE											
		0	1	2	3	4	5	6	7	8	9	A	B
ACTIONS	0	0	0	0	0	0	0	0	0	0	0	0	0
	1	-3	+2	+2	+2	+2	+2	+2	+2	+2	+2	+1·5	+1·5
	2	-6	-1	+4	+4	+4	+4	+4	+4	+4	+4	+2·5	+2·5
	3	-9	-4	+1	+6	+6	+6	+6	+6	+6	+6	+3	+3
	4	-12	-7	-2	+3	+8	+8	+8	+8	+8	+8	+3	+2·5
	5	-15	-10	-5	0	+5	+10	+10	+10	+10	+10	+2·5	+1
	6	-18	-13	-8	-3	+2	+7	+12	+12	+12	+12	+1·5	-1·5
	7	-21	-16	-11	-6	-1	+4	+9	+14	+14	+14	0	-4·25
	8	-24	-19	-14	-9	-4	+1	+6	+11	+16	+16	-2	-7·15
	9	-27	-22	-17	-12	-7	-2	+3	+8	+13	+18	-4·5	-10·1

Figure 1 (a) Profit and Loss Consequences Table

for each combination of his choice of stock level with the demand which might occur.

(iv) There is a criterion on the basis of which the action may be chosen. This may take a variety of forms, according to the trading philosophy of the bookseller. He may say that the maximum loss he is prepared to risk is £10, and subject to that he wishes to take action which has the greatest profit possibility. Then, by reference to Figure 1(a), we would advise him to set up a stock of 3 books; any greater number exposes him to a risk of losing more than £10; no smaller number offers the possibility of a profit as great as £6.

In each of the foregoing paragraphs (i) to (iv), we implied that the given conditions were not the only ones possible. The coronation souvenir problem is, in fact, just one of a wide range of problems constituting the subject of stock planning. Related problems abound. For example, a hospital pharmacist must maintain stocks of life-saving drugs, but must be careful that rapid advances of medical technique do not leave him with enormous quantities of a drug which has suddenly been superseded. Or, again, a storeman in an engineering works who maintains a stock of mechanical spare parts always wishes to be able to supply the very part which may be needed to repair important productive machinery, but certainly does not wish to be burdened with the task of looking after tens of thousands of spares each of which may be required no more than once every three years.

Anyone who acquires a stock of a commodity in order to supply it to others we shall call a 'stockist'; his decision problem – how large a stock to hold – we shall call, in its most general terms, 'the stockist's problem'; and any solution to this problem we shall call the 'policy stock'. We shall analyse a few of the more frequently encountered versions of the stockist's problem, building upon the coronation souvenir example, varying the conditions of the problem and showing how, in each case, we can determine an appropriate policy stock.

COMPLEXITY OF CONSEQUENCE

In the coronation souvenir example, we can readily draw up a table of profit and loss consequences for each choice of stock level and each demand which might occur. The only relevant data are the buying and selling value of the book.

Often, things are a good deal more complicated than this. For example, without departing from the problem of a once-only decision, we may consider the problem of a dealer in government surplus equipment who is offered a single opportunity of buying lots of 10,000 each of surplus batteries which have a shelf life of one year, provided they are recharged every month. At the end of the year, he can sell them for scrap at a much reduced price, but whilst he keeps them he is incurring a cost for looking after them. They take up valuable space and must be inspected and maintained.*

In estimating the consequences of each action and state of nature which can occur in a stock planning problem, therefore, it is necessary to identify *all* the elements which are relevant. For example, in acquiring the stock there may be problems of handling or delivery; there may be discount prices for quantity; there may be administrative problems associated with raising the order. In storing the stock there may be problems of obsolescence, inspection or maintenance; special environmental conditions, such as refrigeration, may be required; it may be necessary to accommodate the stock in rented warehouse space; the stock may shrink, dry out or evaporate with time. The consequence of too much stock may be an expensive disposal problem, or it may be that the stock can readily be sold for scrap; the consequence of too little stock may be the loss of further orders from a good customer, or it may mean the expensive rushing of emergency supplies from some other source.†

* There is also, of course, the opportunity cost of the capital tied up in stock. This represents the 'cost' of the rate of return which is foregone by using the capital to hold stock instead of investing the money in some alternative opportunity. In theory, the opportunity cost must at least cover the cost at the cutoff rate. See George Taylor's discussion of the cost of capital in Part III.

† In some instances the problems of insufficient stock to meet required demand may be catastrophic: e.g. insufficient weapons to win a war; insufficient monitors to predict an earthquake, typhoon, tornado, tidal wave; insufficient drugs to combat an epidemic; insufficient parts to keep equipment operational such as in a computer or early-warning device.

In considering further examples of the stockist's problem, therefore, we shall assume that, in drawing up a consequences table such as that of Figure 1(*a*), the stockist has identified the penalties and advantages of the *whole* operation – getting the stock, holding it and disposing of it.

DIVERSITY OF CRITERIA

In drawing up his table of consequences, we have said, the stockist must include everything which is 'relevant'. The question – what is relevant? – is related to the stockist's choice of *criterion* as a decision-maker. In the coronation souvenir example, we assumed a particular trading philosophy for the bookseller. Many others are possible;* for example, Figure 1(*b*) shows for the same problem the 'regret' associated with each combination of choice and outcome – i.e. the amount by which the bookseller is financially worse off than he would have been if he had set up exactly the right stock to match the state of nature which occurred. A bookseller whose philosophy is to hedge against regret will seek the action for which the regret, in the worst possible outcome, is as little as possible. By reference to Figure 1(*b*), we would advise him to set a stock of three or four books; any other choice exposes him to the possibility of a regret greater than £12.

Again, the bookseller may wish to base his actions, not upon worst or best possible outcomes, but upon 'expected', (average) outcomes – he may wish, for instance, to choose the action for which the average profit is greatest. Here we must make an assumption, in default of information to the contrary, that each of the possible 'states of nature' is equally likely. Then the average profits are as shewn in Column 'A' of Figure 1(*a*), and we would again advise him to set up a stock of three or four books.

Finally, the bookseller may work on a criterion of 'customer

---

* See the range of philosophies examined in D. W. Miller and M. K. Starr, *Executive Decisions and Operations Research*, ch. 5 (Prentice-Hall, 1960).

service', because he does not wish to acquire a reputation for disappointing his customers. He may wish to choose an action from which he will not incur a risk greater than one-in-ten of being unable to meet the demand. A stockist who operates this criterion in a once-only decision is likely

ACTIONS	STATES OF NATURE									
	0	1	2	3	4	5	6	7	8	9
0	0	2	4	6	8	10	12	14	16	18
1	3	0	2	4	6	8	10	12	14	16
2	6	3	0	2	4	6	8	10	12	14
3	9	6	3	0	2	4	6	8	10	12
4	12	9	6	3	0	2	4	6	8	10
5	15	12	9	6	3	0	2	4	6	8
6	18	15	12	9	6	3	0	2	4	6
7	21	18	15	12	9	6	3	0	2	4
8	24	21	18	15	12	9	6	3	0	2
9	27	24	21	18	15	12	9	6	3	0

Figure 1(b) Regret Consequences Table

to make a loss; but he may consider that this is a reasonable trading cost, which keeps his customers loyal and so ensures that he takes profits elsewhere. Assuming again that demands of zero, one, two, . . ., nine are all equally likely, we would advise such a stockist to set up a stock of eight books, so that only the one-in-ten chance of a demand for nine will cause him to disappoint a customer. On the evidence, this will expose him to an expected loss of £2, as column 'A' of Figure 1(a) shows.

THE VALUE OF INFORMATION

One of the difficulties of the once-only decision problem is a lack of information, causing us to *guess* that all the states of nature are equally likely. This may be far from the truth, and it may pay the bookseller in the coronation souvenir example to do some market research before making a decision. Suppose, then, that he makes a telephone survey. He pays a research company to ring up a selected sample of residents in the area of his shop, to inquire whether they would be interested in buying the souvenir. The research company adjusts the results of the inquiry by relating it to a forecast of the number of shoppers who will visit the shop during the relevant period, and on the basis of this they present the following information, organized into a 'Demand Probability Table':

X: States of nature [Possible number of books to be sold]	0	1	2	3	4	5	6	7	8	9
P: % Probability of actual number sold exceeding X	90	80	70	50	30	10	5	2	1	0

Figure 2. *Demand Probability Table*

This table shows that the survey indicates that the bookseller has only a fifty-fifty chance of selling more than three books, and his chances of selling more than six are as little as one-in-twenty (5%). The first question which suggests itself is – how reliable is this information? This question can, in fact, be given a precise mathematical form, and estimates of the reliability of information can be brought into the analysis of the stockist's problem.* For our present purposes, however, this would take us rather too far afield, and we

* For an exposition of the sampling problems involved, see Slonim (ed. Yewdall), *op. cit.*, ch. 18 and especially pages 110–15.

will assume that the information in Figure 2 is, in an intuitive sense, 'reliable'.

In that case, the likely demand is on the low side, and this information materially affects the stockist's decision. For example, the average profit associated with a decision to stock four books is not in fact £3, as in the fifth row of column A of the consequences table of Figure 1(a), but is rather

$$£\{-12(1\cdot0-0\cdot9) -7(0\cdot9-0\cdot8) -2(0\cdot8-0\cdot7) + 3(0\cdot7-0\cdot5) + 8 \times 0\cdot5\}$$

$$= £2\cdot5$$

as in column B.*

In the same way, the average profit associated with each action can be adjusted to give the rest of column B in Figure 1(a), from which it will be seen that a bookseller using the criterion of greatest average profit should now choose a stock of three books, giving him an expected profit of £3. Had he not purchased the extra information, the bookseller might have opted for four books, with, as we now see, an expected profit of 10/– less.

Again, if he is working to the criterion of customer service, he now knows that a stock of five books is adequate to reduce his risk of giving disappointment to as little as 10%. Had he worked on his previous assumption that all states of nature were equally likely, he would have set up a stock of eight books, and would have exposed himself to an expected loss of £7·15 instead of an expected profit of £1. Hence, if his market intelligence cost him less than £8·15 he has done well.

* This expected average value is obtained by taking the value of each outcome and multiplying it by the individual probability of each event: e.g. the probability of *exactly* five books sold is the probability of more than four minus the probability of more than five ($= 0\cdot3-0\cdot1 = 0\cdot2$) which is then multiplied by the value of five sales (£10). The sum of all such possibilities produces the expected average value for each possible action. This type of calculation is demonstrated step by step in the work cited in the footnote reference on page 119.

Chapter Fifteen

THE RECURRENT DECISION

WE can summarize our discussion of the once-only stockist's problem by saying that a policy stock can be calculated, once the philosophy of the stockist is known, by using devices such as the consequences table and the demand probability table. The consequences table can be arrived at by a thorough review, but the demand probability table is difficult to come by, and the goodness of the information it contains materially affects the goodness of the decision.

Things are a great deal easier, however, if the stockist's problem is recurrent. For example, consider how the problem is changed if the commodities being stocked are newspapers, or pastries. As in the coronation souvenir problem, the economic value of the commodity after the day of sale is greatly reduced, but instead of the operation being conducted once only, it is conducted anew every day, so that a good deal of statistical evidence is available on the basis of which more reliable decisions can be made. Instead of one-time prediction based upon market research, the stockist can appeal to *past experience* to show what proportion of the time the demand reaches any assigned level.

For example, suppose that a newsagent keeps a record, for a hundred consecutive days, of the demand he experiences for a particular newspaper. He may count the number of days on which the demand exceeds 10, the number on which it exceeds 20, 30, and so on, and express this data as a table:

X: Demand	0	10	20	30	40	50	60	70	80	90
P: No. of days on which demand exceeds X	100	100	95	90	80	65	50	35	10	0

Figure 3. *Statistical Demand Data*

This, of course, is a Demand Probability Table, such as that of Figure 2; but based upon actual experience rather than market research. We may use it in exactly the same way to advise the stockist, according to his trading philosophy, what his policy stock should be. Thus, a stockist whose criterion is a one-in-ten risk of failing to give customer service, sets a policy stock of 80; he places a standing order with the newspaper publisher for 80 copies a day.

TIME SERIES

But we must examine this decision a little further. If he is wise,* the newsagent will take a sheet of graph paper, mark the days from one to 100 along the bottom and plot the actual demand, as shown in Figure 4. Such a graph is called a *time series*. If the appearance is as in Figure 4(a), then the foregoing argument is sound. The experience shows an average daily demand for 57 papers, with the demand never falling below 10 and never rising above 90, and a policy stock of 80 will indeed ensure that only on one day in ten will demand exceed supply.

If, however, the graph presents the appearance of Figure

* Although the editor has occasionally had the experience that students of management science were able to try out their ideas in a small shop or small business context, it would be unusual for a newsagent himself to be thoroughly conversant with these techniques. Dr Cuninghame-Green is really using the newsagent's as a simple business situation for purposes of demonstrating the planning techniques which are available to cope with changes in the level of demand. These techniques are applicable to any size of business operation.

4(b), things are very different. The market is growing, and much of the information buried in the table of Figure 3 is rather out-of-date. There is, in fact, a much greater likelihood of demand exceeding 80 than Figure 3 would suggest. If we look at the graph, we see that the policy stock level

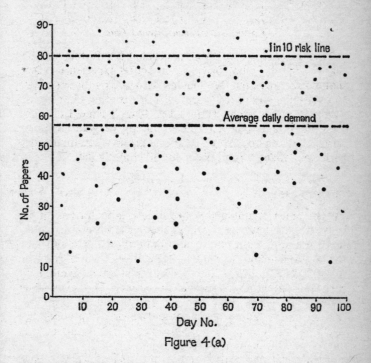

Figure 4(a)

which suits this particular stockist's philosophy steadily rises. Fifty weeks ago, a level which was likely to be exceeded only one time in ten was somewhere round the 70 mark; now it would be close to 100.

This complication is readily dealt with. The solid line on the graph is drawn to represent the general movement of the market. We can call this the 'Market Index', and in the case of Figure 4(*b*), the stockist can readily draw a reasonably accurate market index line by eye. He will observe that the actual demand never, or rarely, actually falls on the market index line, but falls in a fairly random pattern above or below it. If he re-examines his 100 days' experience

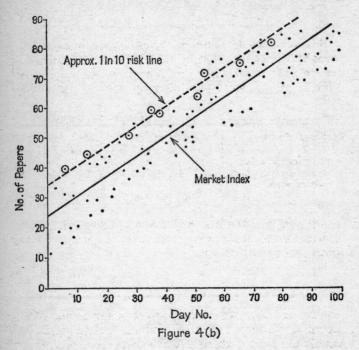

Figure 4(b)

in relation to the market index he will find, say, that actual demand never falls below the index by more than 16, and never falls above the index by more than 19. Extending this line of thought, he can draw up a demand probability table as before, expressed not in absolute terms, but in terms *relative to the market index*, with the 'states of nature' now being the actual demands expressed in terms of the value of the market index at the time of the demand:

X: States of nature	Index −16	Index −11	Index −6	Index −1	Index +4	Index +9	Index +14	Index +19
P: No. of occasions on which Actual demand exceeds X	100	90	70	50	30	10	5	0

He would then use this in the following way. By extending the solid line on the graph by one day, he would arrive at a forecast of the market index for tomorrow – say 92. On this basis he would derive the following demand probability table:

X: States of nature	76	81	86	91	96	101	106	111
P: % Probability that tomorrow's demand will exceed X	100	90	70	50	30	10	5	0

And then, in the light of his individual trading philosophy, he would arrive at his policy stock for tomorrow, using the arguments already discussed.

ROUTINE STOCK PLANNING

The process described in the preceding section is fundamental to the subject of stock planning, and we may now identify the basic mechanics of solving the recurring stockist's problem as we have so far described it:

(i) Draw up a consequences table, based upon a thorough review of the consequences of each decision and each state of nature.

(ii) By reviewing a suitably large period of the recent history of the demand for the product, identify a market index which follows the general movement of the market.

(iii) By looking at the actual history of demand in relation to the market index, form a demand probability table in terms relative to the index.

(iv) Forecast the movement of the market index tomorrow.

(v) Apply the relative demand probability table to the forecast, to arrive at a specific demand probability table for the next decision.

(vi) Use this specific demand probability table, in conjunction with the consequences table, in solving the stockist's problem relative to his individual criterion.*

(vii) When the new demand actually materializes, add the experience of it to the record; for the next decision, repeat steps (i) to (vi), making use of the new information.

In the example considered, a suitable index was taken to be a straight line drawn by eye through the middle of the points on the time series, and the forecasting was reduced to a simple extrapolation of this line. For many day-to-day purposes with cheap commodities and reliable markets, such methods work tolerably well. But for many other cases this would be impossibly crude, and more sophisticated methods are called for; and this introduces a new question – the economics of the stock planning process itself. Elaborate systems of stock planning involve substantial amounts of calculation, which typically must be performed either by a clerk or by a computer. There is no point in using expensive methods to make cheap decisions, and if the cost of storing the necessary information and making the necessary calculations exceeds the value of making good stock decisions, then the effort is misapplied.

The stockist's first step, then, before setting up a routine system to solve his problem, should be to review his histori-

* The reader will find a more rapid method of calculating the optimum stock level by reference to the Critical Ratio given in Schlaifer, *op. cit.*, ch . 4.

cal records to estimate the value to himself of making better stock decisions. Suppose the newsagent, for example, draws up a record of:

(a) The demand which actually occurred on the last 100 occasions,
(b) The stocks which he actually provided on each occasion,
(c) The stocks which he *would* have provided had he been using the proposed method of calculation.

On the basis of this data, he can decide, according to his own criterion, whether the stock control system is worth the trouble. If he operates according to a criterion of maximum average profit, for example, he can see whether the gain in average annual profit as a result of a more scientific régime of stock planning would actually repay the cost of the control system.

The decision as to whether to set up a crude or an elaborate system of stock planning therefore depends upon the stockist's individual philosophy; but, generally speaking, the areas where elaborate methods of stock planning are likely to pay off include: those where the commodity being stocked is expensive but perishable, or vulnerable to changes of fashion; those where the commodity is expensive to store because of awkward shape, low volume density or need for refrigeration; those where the stock is financed by short-term capital bearing heavy interest rates; those where a very wide range of commodities are handled, so that small inefficiencies on each can amount to an important total; those where running out of stock has important consequences, such as loss of business. In such cases, the penalty of overstocking or understocking can be substantial, and an effective method of stock planning well worth the effort. We shall return later to the question of how the stock planning routine fits into the organization of the stockist's business.

EXPONENTIAL SMOOTHING

In order to develop the subject a step further, let us take the case of a dealer in fruit, vegetables and flowers, who owns a chain of retail stores which he stocks with fresh goods from the market every morning. Because his goods are not cheap, and are highly perishable, he decides, let us say, that it is worth his while employing a clerk to spend a few hours

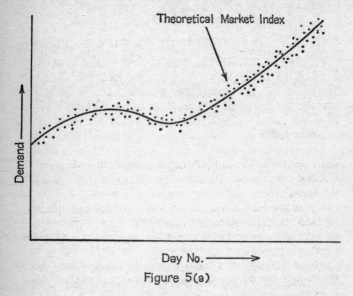

Figure 5(a)

each day planning the stock he should set up for each of his more important lines in each of his shops. When the clerk comes to draw the time series of demand for, say, apples, he may find an expanding market, as did the newsagent. However, instead of the idealized pattern of regular growth assumed in Figure 4(b) for purposes of simplicity in introducing the idea of a market index, the clerk is more likely in practice to find something on the lines of Figure 5(a). The problem is to find a practical way of plotting a market index when the simple process of drawing a straight line is inapplicable. One way of doing this is by use of a *moving average:* each day, the clerk computes the average of the most recent ten, say, of his days' sales, and uses this as an index of the current state of the market.

The use of moving averages involves quite a lot of book-keeping. In the case considered, the clerk must keep a book of his last ten days' sales for each line in each shop; each day he adds a new day's experience to the record, deletes the oldest item from the record, takes the average of the ten and uses this as his index to the market. A slightly more convenient procedure than this involves a technique called 'exponential smoothing'. The clerk merely keeps a record, the index itself, and then when the actual sales are known on a given day the new value of the index is calculated as the average of the old index and the new demand. Thus:

New index = $\frac{1}{2}$ (Old index) + $\frac{1}{2}$ (Today's Demand)

$$- (1)$$

Now, since the 'old index' was yesterday's 'new index',

Old index = $\frac{1}{2}$ (Previous old index) + $\frac{1}{2}$ (Yesterday's Demand)

and Previous old index = $\frac{1}{2}$ (Next-previous old index) + $\frac{1}{2}$ (Day before yesterday's Demand)

etc., etc.

It follows, then, that

New index = $\frac{1}{2}$ (Today's Demand) + $\frac{1}{4}$ (Yesterday's Demand) + $\frac{1}{8}$ (Day before yesterday's demand) + ... etc.

$$- (2)$$

Thus, the market index produced by exponential smoothing is compounded out of the whole demand history of the commodity, but the more out-of-date information is in effect given less and less weight in calculating the index. It is for these reasons that exponential smoothing suggests itself as a method of forming an index – it is sensitive to changes in the market because it gives greater weight to more recent experience, but it does reflect, in a stable market, the long-term average demand.

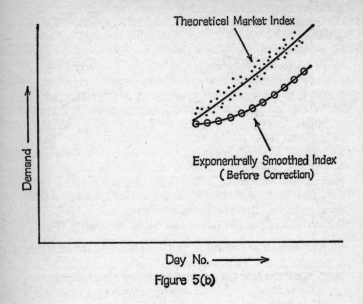

Figure 5(b)

PROPERTIES OF THE INDEX

Exponential smoothing is slightly more general than we have suggested. If, instead of equation (1), we had written

New index = $\frac{9}{10}$ (Old index) + $\frac{1}{10}$ (Today's demand),

then instead of equation (2), we should have

New index = $\frac{1}{10}$ (Today's demand) + $\frac{9}{100}$ (Yesterday's Demand) + $\frac{81}{1000}$ (Day before Yesterday's Demand) + . . . etc.

Such an index puts almost equal weight upon each item of the demand experience, and gives a smooth indication of the long-term average level of a stable market. This is illustrated in Figure 6(a), where the index is used with part of the data of Figure 4(a) – the demand for newspapers. However, if the market conditions changed, and demand began growing, this index would be very slow to respond because it

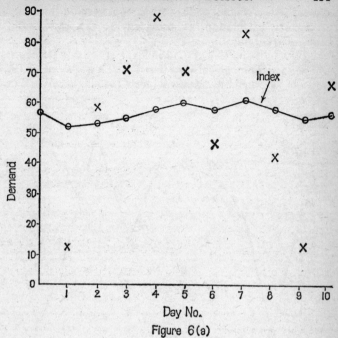

Figure 6(a)

would still be reflecting the distant past. If we want an index which is sensitive to change, we might try:

New index = $\frac{1}{10}$ (Old index) + $\frac{9}{10}$ (Today's Demand),

which is of the same basic form, but puts nine times as much weight on the new data as on the old index. For this:

New index = $\frac{9}{10}$ (Today's Demand) + $\frac{9}{100}$ (Yesterday's Demand) + $\frac{9}{1000}$ (Day before Yesterday's Demand) + ... etc.

If we apply this index to the same data, however, we produce a very 'ragged' effect, because the index is sensitive to individual high demand and ceases to reflect the general market average, as Figure 6(b) shows.

Summing this up, then, we may say that a convenient

market index which requires little bookkeeping and only elementary calculation, is provided by the exponential smoothing formula:

New index $= (1-\alpha)$ (Old index) $+\alpha$(Today's Demand)

where α is a number between 0 and 1. If α is chosen small, (say $\alpha = \frac{1}{10}$), then the index will reflect the long-term market

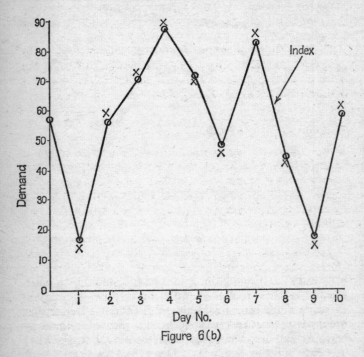

Figure 6(b)

average but will be relatively insensitive to change, while if α is chosen large (say $\alpha = \frac{9}{10}$) then the index will be sensitive to change but will behave in a 'ragged' unstable way, making the process of forecasting difficult.

Two further questions we may ask of this index are – how does it respond to a growing market such as that of Figure 5(a)?; and what process do we use to forecast its movement tomorrow, in accordance with step (iv) of the routine stock planning process of page 126? Figure 5(*b*) illustrates the answer to the first question; the market index responds correctly to the rate of climb of the market, but unfortunately lags behind it in time. To correct this, it is necessary to make the definition of the market index rather more complicated; and the second question – forecasting the movement of the index tomorrow – adds a further complication.

The Appendix shows the formulae finally arrived at. In complexity, these approach perhaps the limit of what can conveniently be operated routinely on a manual basis as a practical market index and forecast.

THE SEASONAL PRODUCT

If the commodity which the stockist sells is ice-cream, a time-series showing the demand he experiences over, say, 100 consecutive weeks will probably look rather like that of Figure 7(*a*). The use of exponential smoothing to give a market index for a seasonal product of this kind is not very satisfactory, since the turn-down of trade following the seasonal peak would not affect the index sufficiently quickly.

Various schemes are available as alternatives. One of these works with a 'seasonal profile', showing what proportion of a year's demand falls into each period of the year. Figure 7(*b*) shows such a profile for a year divided into 13 accounting periods of four weeks each. Each year, this profile is revised in the light of the previous year's experience, and each week (say) an estimate of a whole year's demand is made by an exponential smoothing method. By applying this estimate to the most up-to-date version of the profile, a forecast can be made of the demand falling in each future period.

A more sophisticated method consists of finding a mathematical formula which, as nearly as possible, matches the time-series. For example, the solid line of Figure 7(*a*) is given by a mathematical formula of a standard kind. As this line follows the general shape of time series fairly well, it can be used as a market index, and by evaluating the formula against tomorrow's date, it can be used to give a forecast of the future movement of the index. This technique is discussed further in the Appendix.

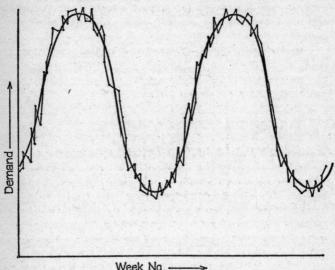

Figure 7(a) Seasonal Demand

SUMMARY ON THE MARKET INDEX

Starting with the once-only decision, we have shown how the Demand Probability Table is used in solving the stockist's problem. For the recurrent decision, we showed how the use of a market index enables us to forecast the Demand Probability Table afresh each time a stock decision is required. With a relatively steady demand, such as that shown in Figure 4(a) one can then calculate the policy stock once, and keep to it, merely checking at intervals to ensure that the market still remains steady.

With a changing market, such as that shown in Figure 4(*b*), exponential smoothing may be used, and the Demand Probability Table constructed, using the formulae in the Appendix. For a stockist with a relatively small range of items, this procedure can be operated manually on a routine basis.

With seasonal markets, more calculation is necessary,

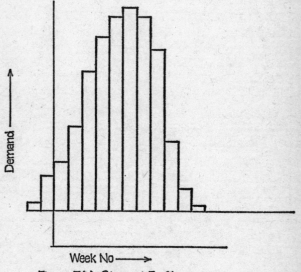

Figure 7(b) Seasonal Profile

and a stockist who stocks a large number of different commodities, with many seasonal items, is likely to require a computer for sophisticated stock planning calculations. A stockist who contemplates using a computer for his financial and stock accounting processes is well placed to build the stock planning calculations into these processes. The history of stock transactions – orders, deliveries, requisitions, physical stock counts, sales – will flow through the files of his computer accounting system and provide simultaneously the necessary raw materials for computerized stock planning decisions.

The mechanics of stock planning may therefore fit into the stockist's organization in a variety of ways, according to circumstances. We shall enlarge upon this point when we come to consider the multi-item stockist's problem. Before this we must extend the scope of the discussion to other aspects of the stockist's problem, so far unconsidered.

Chapter Sixteen

ADDITIONAL COMPLEXITIES

TOP-UP SYSTEMS

IN order to advance the argument one step at a time, our treatment so far of the recurrent stockist's problem has assumed that each day's decision is self-contained. The stock is created as required for the start of the day, and at the end any which is unused cannot be carried forward to the morrow. Each day's decision stands or falls on its own, and only *information* is carried forward.

If the commodity is of a type, however, whose economic value does *not* disappear at the end of the day, a different situation emerges. Consider, for example, the stocks of linen on a hospital ward: any not used today can be used tomorrow. We may calculate the demand probability table by using the foregoing arguments, and on the basis of that, determine the policy stock. The question now is whether the stock on hand any morning is above or below the policy stock level. If above, no supplies are requisitioned; if below, enough is requisitioned to bring the level up to the policy stock level.

Such a method of stock administration is sometimes called a 'top-up system'. If the demand is relatively stable (as in Figure 4(*a*)), then the policy stock level can be fixed for reasonably long periods of time. Under these circumstances, the simple rule of stock planning becomes: 'requisition today the amount you used yesterday'.

THE LEAD TIME

In the examples so far considered, we have assumed that

supplies are available every morning, for the stockist to make up his stocks. His only problem is to decide how much to take. Very often, however, a stockist does not find himself in that position, and must take account of the fact that a significant time must elapse between his taking a stock planning decision, and his receiving supplies.

For example, consider the problem of a trader who deals in a fabric which is supplied direct from a factory at the other end of the country; or an engineering accessories shop which handles sub-assemblies which will have to be specially made at the factory. In such cases, the stockist must reckon on a delay between the moment when he asks for supplies and the moment when he receives them. This delay is known as the 'Lead Time'.

The existence of a lead time affects the stockist's problem very materially. When he reviews his stock, he must argue as follows: 'If I do not order any fresh supplies today, then the stock which I have now will have to last until the next time I review the stock, *plus* the lead time which must then ensue.' This total period – lead time plus interval between reviews – we may call 'the vulnerable period'.

The stockist's problem now is – what is an appropriate stock with which to enter the vulnerable period? Essentially, this is a repetition of the stockist's problem in the form in which we have already considered it, except that instead of demand-during-a-day we must consider demand-during-a-vulnerable-period.

Suppose, for example, that a grocer reviews his stock every week, and that it takes his wholesaler three days to deliver whatever he orders. Then ten days is his vulnerable period. To set up a stock planning system for him, we would study a time series, not of daily demand, but of demand-during-ten-consecutive-days. We would then follow out the procedures of our earlier discussion, arriving, according to the criterion of the stockist, at a policy stock for him to apply on each review day. If his existing stock is greater than the policy stock, he does not order; if it is less, he orders enough to bring it up to policy level.

A small modification is necessary to the foregoing statement to give it more general validity. In the example we chose, the lead time was less than the interval between stock reviews, but the reverse could well be the case. If this occurs, it is possible that at the time of stock review some supplies are already on order, from a previous review, but not yet delivered. Since these supplies will arrive some time during the current lead time, they must be credited to the stock when comparing it to the policy stock. The term 'virtual stock' is sometimes used to cover 'stock on hand plus stock on order'. In general, then, the stockist places an order whenever, at review times:

> 'Virtual stock' is less than 'policy-stock-for-vulnerable-period'.

Of course, lead times are by no means always constant. The mathematical theory of stock planning readily accommodates the extra complexity of variable lead time, and the discussion of the general problem above does not need to assume a fixed lead time.*

EMERGENCY ORDERS

A policy stock may be calculated in relation to the lead time itself as well as to the total vulnerable period. If, when the stockist makes his review, he finds that his virtual stock has fallen below policy-stock-for-lead-time, there is in theory nothing he can do. He is probably going to run into understock penalties, since by definition he cannot get further supplies sooner than one lead time.

If, however, the supplier is prepared to produce 'rush orders', but at a premium price to cover the inconvenience, the case is altered. Suppose that the stockist, using the criterion of maximum expected profit, finds that his policy stock level in relation to one lead time should be four

* Variable lead time is covered in the literature referenced at the end of the Appendix; see especially the work by Miller and Starr (reference 8) and by Whitin (reference 9).

crates of a particular commodity. His normal consequences table may look as follows:

No. of crates in stock	0	1	2	3	4	5	6	7
Expected profit	£0	£4	£7	£8	£9	£8 15 –	£8 10 –	£8

Suppose that the supplier is always prepared to provide rush orders, but at an extra cost of 30/– per crate. Clearly, the stockist will not make use of this facility if the gain in expected profit which accrues to him on any crate so ordered is less than 30/–. Thus, in the example under consideration, if his virtual stock at the review time were 2, 3 or 4 crates, he would not place a rush order.* If it were zero or one crate, he would place a rush order to bring the virtual stock up to 2. Any further order would cost him 30/– per crate extra, and enhance his expected profit by £1 per case or less. From this discussion, it follows that the same apparatus – consequences table and demand probability table – can be applied to demand-during-a-lead-time to define an *emergency order level*, as distinct from the *routine order level* previously considered.

Hence, we can provide the stockist with two critical levels; if his virtual stock is greater than the routine order level, he does not place an order; if it lies below the routine order level but above the emergency order level, he places a routine order; if it lies below the emergency order level, he places a rush order.

(s,s) AND EOQ

Our discussion of policy stock and top-up systems has set

* This is not, of course, paying any regard to the value which the stockist might place on the goodwill of a particular customer for whom the rush order would be requested. In this latter case there would be tradeoff between the value placed on the customer's goodwill and the incremental loss on the rush order.

the stage for two celebrated ideas of classical stock planning theory. The first of these is the so-called '(S,s) policy' of stock management, according to which the stockist specifies two numbers, S and s, with $0 < s < S$; when he reviews stock, he orders only if his stock has fallen below level s, and then he orders enough to bring it up to level S.

This policy is mentioned here because it is an intuitively plausible one which is sometimes taken to be self-evidently efficient. But it is clear that unless the demand exhibits the stable characteristics of Figure 4(a), the quantities s and S are unlikely to remain constant through time. A number of studies have been made of the conditions under which the (S,s) policy is, in fact, optimal, and have revealed that even in quite simple stock problems the (S,s) form of stock planning rule is often not the best.

And a practical problem raised by the (S,s), and indeed all the systems discussed so far is the assumption that supplies can be ordered in arbitrary amounts – perhaps five today, perhaps five hundred next week. In the classical top-up system, this might be possible; but in many contexts it is hardly likely that a supplier will undertake to supply in such an irregular fashion, nor that the stockist will find it economical or convenient to handle supplies in such varying amounts.

On the basis of these considerations, a classical argument computes an *Economic Order Quantity* – (EOQ) – a standard amount which strikes an economic balance among the costs of placing an order, handling the quantity ordered and storing it until it has been issued. The analysis is shown in the Appendix. The EOQ is a useful notion, but its application requires care. First of all, whilst it is certainly relevant to the stockist who handles one item only, its use to cover the case of a stockist who handles many items becomes problematical. Secondly, the EOQ often turns out to be an amount which, whilst theoretically optimal, is of an awkward size practically. And thirdly, the pay-off from the EOQ is often very small, in the sense that a policy of ordering amounts which are not too different from the EOQ is often very nearly as efficient.

In practice, therefore, the amount ordered is likely to be dictated by other considerations – a convenient amount to handle, an amount which secures best discount terms, an amount which can readily be accommodated, and so on.

THE MULTI-ITEM CASE – A SYNTHESIS

By way of a review and summary of the ideas we have discussed, let us consider how a stockist who handles a wide variety of different commodities, from different manufacturers, with different lead times and different markets, might go about a comprehensive system of stock planning.

His first task is to classify the items he controls. Since his aim is to set up a routine system of the kind described above, he must first define those items to which such a system would *not* apply. These are of two kinds – those where an expensive system is not justified for making cheap decisions, and those where a system, no matter how expensive, is no substitute for direct management supervision.

Into the first category come any items for which the penalties associated with a bad stock decision are trivial. If *understock* penalties are trivial, then the stockist should consider giving up stocking the item, merely ordering against actual demand. If *overstock* penalties are trivial, as with a cheap easily stored commodity (e.g. iron nails), then a '2-bin' system is appropriate. Two bulk stocks are kept, each containing an amount which is large compared with the demand-during-a-lead-time. As soon as one is used up, the other is broached and an order placed for a new 'binful'.

Into the second category come any items for which the penalties associated with bad stock decisions are very high. These are the items which the stockist wishes to keep under surveillance and not delegate the control to a clerical or automatic process. He requires *management information* rather than automatic control. He should set up a communications system which feeds him timely and accurate information on the state of the market, the recent demand figures, the availability of supplies, the stock on hand and on order, and any other intelligence which is likely to bear upon the problem – the political situation, the availability of money, the likely imposition of taxes and duties, the weather forecast, or whatever may be relevant. It is likely that he would, in fact, set up a routine system, but it would be one which would supply *suggested* decisions to him, rather than one to which he delegated authority for taking decisions.

Between these extremes, as it were, fall the commodities for which the stockist is likely to see a pay-off from the introduction of a routine control system. Those for which demand is relatively stable, he can determine his policy stock level from the history of recent demand; he will review it occasionally, but does not need to establish computational routines. Those for which demand is increasing or decreasing fairly uniformly, a market index can be set up and updated as a routine clerical procedure, and policy stock levels recomputed at each stock review. If the stockist handles a wide range of commodities, having irregular growth patterns, and seasonal characteristics, the computation of market indices and policy stock levels becomes a more elaborate process suitable for integration into a computerized stock accounting system.

The use of a routine system, either clerical or automatic, is very naturally done on a 'management by exception' basis. Since the calculations determine a routine reorder level and an emergency reorder level, a natural arrangement is for the stockist to delegate to the clerical or automatic process the ordering of further supplies when stocks fall to the routine reorder level, but to set up information channels to tell him if ever stocks fall to the emergency level.

From this point of view, stock planning can be regarded as a system of planned delegation of decision-making, as Figure 8 illustrates; the setting up of automatic systems does not aim to substitute for the process of management, but rather to prevent the overmanagement of run-of-the-mill situations, and so make possible the detailed management of the exceptions.

TYPE A: High penalties. Minimal delegation. Premium placed on accurate and timely management information.

TYPE B: Medium penalties. Delegation on a 'management by exception' basis, to automatic or clerical procedures.

TYPE C: Low penalties. Maximum delegation. Minimal investment in control procedures.

Figure 8. *Delegation of Stock Planning*

INTERACTING ITEMS

In discussing the multi-item situation, we assumed that the stockist would solve his problem for each item individually and independently. This might not be practicable. For example, if the stockist holds all his items in the same warehouse, he must take care that the total of the policy stocks he calculates is not greater than he can accommodate in the warehouse.

Again, a stockist who operates according to the criterion of customer service might nevertheless not be prepared to hold unreasonably large stocks so as to give a virtually perfect service. In deciding what policy level to set, he may make an analysis to see what capital investment he has been in the habit of making in stocks in the past, and decide that he will replan his stocks, so as to continue to make the capital commitment he is now adjusted to, but also to give the lowest level of risk of customer disappointment over the whole range of items.

These two problems are abstractly identical; they involve the sharing of a fixed resource – space or capital – over a number of items, for each of which the individual rate of exchange between the use of the resource and the achievement of the stockist's aim, is known. And they are, moreover, abstractly identical to a third important problem of stock management, which we may call the 'distributor's problem'.

If a stockist has a central stock of a commodity, which he wishes to distribute to a number of field depots, then the sum of the policy stocks he would calculate for each of the field depots may exceed the stock he has, and he must again share out a fixed resource – the stock – to best advantage.

The Appendix shows some of the relevant mathematical theory; the practical procedure to which it gives rise may be illustrated by an example. Suppose a stockist has two field depots, which respectively contain stocks of 64 and 11 crates of a commodity, and that he has an additional central stock of 25 crates which he wishes to share between them. Let the stockist's policy be that of minimizing the expected 'disappointment' to his customers – where the 'disappointment' is the *total* of the amounts by which demand exceeds supply at each depot separately.

[Thus, if stocks were　　　10 and 50
　　　and demands were　　12 and 60
　　　then disappointment is　2 + 10 = 12
whilst, if stocks were　　　10 and 50
　　　and demands were　　12 and 40
　　　then disappointment is　2 + 0 = 2]

Then the stockist forms the demand probability tables for the two depots, using the methods discussed above, and places them side by side, using the same '% probability' scale in both cases, as shown in Figure 9. He adds a further row with the total of the corresponding 'states of nature' as shown. The use of the table is then very simple: if his total available stock is 60, he should divide it 50 : 10; if 67, he should divide it 55 : 12; and so forth.

Intermediate cases are handled by interpolating in the table, which we assume would be drawn up on an appropriately fine scale. In the example chosen, the total stock is 100, which the distributor should divide 80 : 20.

Hence, he sends 16 crates from his central stock to the first depot, and 9 to the second.

The procedure is quite general, and applies (*mutatis mutandis*) to the other equivalent problems of the limited

% Probability that demand exceeds X	90	80	70	60	50	40	30	20	10
X_1: States of nature at first depot	50	55	65	80	100	130	180	250	350
X_2: States of nature at second depot	10	12	15	20	30	50	80	120	180
Total ($X_1 + X_2$)	60	67	80	100	130	180	260	370	530

Figure 9

warehouse space and the fixed capital investment, if the same criterion applies. Other methods are available in the mathematical literature.

THE MANUFACTURER'S PROBLEM

We may mention, in conclusion, the two-fold stock planning problem of the manufacturer of finished goods. First of all, he must plan, on the basis of the arguments we have discussed, the stocks of finished goods he wishes to have, in each of his depots, in each time period of his forward plan, in order to meet the anticipated demand. From this, he must plan his production, using his resources rationally, to produce finished goods stocks which lie within some accepted tolerance of his policy levels.

Secondly, any given production plan constitutes, so to speak, a demand pattern which the manufacturer imposes upon himself as a stockist of the raw materials which he purchases from outside, and in relation to which he must compute his policy stock, having regard to his supplier's lead time.

The details of this total planning exercise are outside the

scope of the present essay, though it is worth remarking that in many cases the planning problem falls into a standard mathematical form – the Linear Program for which standard computer packages are now available.

Chapter Seventeen

MATHEMATICAL APPENDIX

EXPONENTIAL SMOOTHING

The basic process computes

$$\text{New Index} = \alpha\,(\text{Today's Demand}) + (1-\alpha)(\text{Old Index})$$
$$\text{for some } 0 < \alpha < 1.$$

A correction factor is needed to compensate for the lag in responding to trends:

$$\text{Current trend} = \text{New Index} - \text{Old Index}$$

Then

New average trend $= \alpha(\text{Current trend}) + (1-\alpha)(\text{Old average trend})$

This is then used to give

$$\text{Corrected Index} = \text{New Index} + \frac{(1-\alpha)}{\alpha}\,(\text{New average trend})$$

And then a forecast for demand during next L time periods is:

$$L \times \text{Corrected Index} + \frac{L(L+1)}{2} \times \text{New average trend}.$$

GENERAL EXPONENTIAL SMOOTHING

More complex time-series, which exhibit features of seasonality and growth and decay, can often be well represented as linear sums of sinusordal, exponential and polynomial functions of time. General exponential smoothing is a matrix computation for estimating the coefficients of such a model, applying a discount factor to the squared residuals in the regression process so that recent data has more weight than old data. It is fully discussed in (4).

RELATIVE DEMAND DISTRIBUTION

In the text, it was assumed that the demand was related to the market index by an additive error function. In practice, this would need to be determined in each individual case. Where a multiplicative relationship exists, it can be brought to an additive one by use of logarithms.

The relative demand probability table may be handled by a variety of techniques. Where the error distribution is of known (recognizable) type, the parameters will be known functions of the moments, which can be computed by an exponential smoothing procedure:

$$\text{New } n^{th} \text{ moment} = \alpha x^n + (1-\alpha)(\text{Old } n^{th} \text{ moment}).$$

In the common practical case where the error distribution is normal, it is usual to estimate the Mean Absolute Deviation (M·A·D) by

$$\text{New M·A·D} = \alpha \left| (\text{New Deviation}) \right| + (1-\alpha) \text{ Old M·A·D}$$

and then use $\sigma = \sqrt{\dfrac{\pi}{2}} \text{ M·A·D}$

POLICY STOCK IN A COMMON CASE

Under the 'maximum expected profit' or 'minimum expected regret' criterion, and costs which are linear functions of the stock, the optimand can be written:

$$R(X,n) = \alpha_1 X + \beta_1(n) \quad \text{if } n \leqslant X$$
$$\alpha_2 X + \beta_2(n) \quad \text{if } n > X$$

where X is the stock, n is the demand,
and $\alpha_1 X + \beta_1(X) = \alpha_2 X + \beta_2(X)$

If n has cumulative probability function ϕ, then

$$E(R) = \int R\,d\phi$$

$$= \int_{n \le x} [\alpha_1 X + \beta_1(n)]d\phi + \int_{n > x} [\alpha_2 X + \beta_2(n)]d\phi$$

$$\therefore \frac{\partial E}{\partial X} = \alpha_1 \int_{n \le x} d\phi + [\alpha_1 X + \beta_1(X)] \cdot \phi'(X) +$$

$$\alpha_2 \int_{n > x} d\phi - [\alpha_2 X + \beta_2(X)] \cdot \phi'(X)$$

$$= (\alpha_1 - \alpha_2)\int_{n \le x} d\phi + \alpha_2 = -\{(\alpha_2 - \alpha_1)\phi(X) - \alpha_2\}$$

$$\frac{\partial E}{\partial X} = 0 \text{ gives policy stock } \hat{X} = \phi^{-1}\left(\frac{\alpha_2}{\alpha_2 - \alpha_1}\right)$$

ECONOMIC ORDER QUANTITY

A typical E.O.Q. calculation considers:

Cost of raising an order $= a$

Cost of storing one item per unit time $= b$

Demand for item per unit time $= c$

If quantity ordered (E.O.Q.) is x, then:

No. of order raised per unit time $= \dfrac{c}{x}$

Average stock level $= \dfrac{x}{2}$

$\therefore$ Average cost per unit time $= \dfrac{ac}{x} + \dfrac{bx}{2}$

On differentiation, this yields E.O.Q. $= \sqrt{\dfrac{2ac}{b}}$

DISTRIBUTOR'S PROBLEM

The problem of finding non-negative integers $\{x_i\}$, such that

$$\Sigma_1^n x_i = \text{const and } \Sigma_1^n f_i(x_i) = \min$$

for convex $\{f_i\}$, has been solved by O. Gross (see [7]). The routine essentially starts with all $x_i = 0$, then progressively assigns unity to the x_i for which f_i is increasing most slowly. In the example in the text, convexity holds

$$\text{since } \frac{\partial^2}{\partial X^2}\int_x^\infty (n-X)\phi(n)dn = \frac{\partial}{\partial X}\int_x^\infty -\phi(n)dn = \phi(X) \geqslant 0,$$

where X is the stock, n the demand and ϕ the probability density function for n.

REFERENCES

1. K. J. Arrow, T. E. Harris and J. Marschak, 'Optimal inventory policy', *Econometrica*, XIX (1951), 250–72.

2. K. J. Arrow, S. Karlin and H. Scarf, *Studies in the mathematical theory of inventory and production* (Stanford Univ. Press, 1958).

3. R. G. Brown, *Statistical Forecasting for inventory control* (McGraw-Hill, 1959).

4. R. G. Brown, *Smoothing, Forecasting and prediction of discrete time series* (Prentice-Hall, 1962).

5. F. Hanssmann, *Operations Research in Production and Inventory Control* (Wiley, 1962).

6. J. F. Magee, *Production planning and inventory control* (McGraw-Hill, 1958).

7. T. L. Saaty, *Mathematical methods of operations research* (McGraw-Hill, 1959).

8. M. K. Starr and D. W. Miller, *Inventory Control: Theory and Practice* (Prentice-Hall, 1962).

9. T. M. Whitin, *The Theory of Inventory Management* (Princeton Univ. Press, 1957).

10. G. Hadley and T. M. Whitin, *Analysis of Inventory Systems* (Prentice-Hall, 1963).

Part V

MATHEMATICAL AND STATISTICAL FORECASTING

DAVID A. COUTS

President, Palo Alto Research
Associates, Inc., California

David A. Couts graduated B Sc at Queen's University, Belfast, before embarking on four years' work as a petroleum engineer with Imperial Oil Ltd of Canada. He subsequently obtained an M Sc in Operational Research at Birmingham University and then emigrated to America where he obtained his M Sc in Statistics at Stanford University.

After research work on spectral analysis and forecasting economic time series at Stanford, Mr Couts joined the Operations Research staff of Arthur D. Little Inc. There he established an international reputation at forecasting. He developed forecasting techniques as a vital preliminary exercise to production and financial planning for a wide range of activities in transport, wool, timber, water, taxation, petroleum, retailing and engineering.

Mr Couts has contributed important research studies in forecasting, perhaps the two most important being 'Recent Developments in Demand Forecasting', *American Production and Inventory Control Society*, 1966, and 'Forecasting Non-Stationary Economic Time Series', with M. Nerlove and D. Grether, *Management Science*, September 1966.

Recently, David Couts became President of Palo Alto Research Associates, Inc. (PARA), a company which uniquely embodies Mr Couts' own philosophy at applying quantitative techniques to managerial and economic problems in both the private and public sectors.

Chapter Eighteen

WHAT IS FORECASTING?

WHAT IS FORECASTING?

FOR many people, there is a mysteriousness about forecasting. They say, and they are right, that one cannot foretell the future except by a lucky chance or with assistance from the Gods. Faced with a need for forecasts, they may resort to guessing or using rules of thumb. We hope to show that there is a better approach.

Forecasting is estimating. It is understanding a process well enough to be able to describe its important relationships and to estimate the values of its variables. It is neither guessing, nor slavishly applying over-simple rules.

When a building contractor 'estimates' the price for a house, he, in fact, *decides* on a price. He does indeed estimate his cost. He is unlikely to estimate cost with perfect precision, but he understands the limitations of his technique. Accordingly, he decides on a price that he expects will be sufficient to return him a profit, but not so high that his client will choose another contractor.

Estimating the cost of a proposed building may involve estimating the quantities and costs for steel, cement, and other materials, and man hours and wages for various craftsmen and laborers. It may be that a building is so like some others that the cost can be estimated simply, yet accurately, on the basis of square footage and on estimated inflation rates; but usually such gross rules of thumb are unreliable.

Forecasting is necessary. We may be unable to foretell the future, but we do know that it will be affected by past decisions, by decisions about to be made, and by control action about to be taken. Forecasting is the essential basis for decision and control.

Decisions are not frequently repeated, even when they seem to be. Each decision requires a new evaluation of conditions, introduction of new considerations, and often those variables which previously were most important may have become irrelevant. The sets of variables as bases for two decisions are likely to be different. On the other hand, control requires the same set of variables to be continually re-forecast.

Management decides and controls, and has many responsibilities which require both decision and control. Forecasting for control is especially amenable to statistical techniques. Values of a particular set of variables are recorded repeatedly and the variations that occur may be analysed statistically. Decisions, too, are often made with adequate data available for statistical analysis. Frequently, however, they have to be made without the benefit of recorded data, which means without detailed quantitative knowledge of the environment or of the way it tends to vary. Still, mathematical if not statistical analysis can often be used to produce forecasts suitable for guiding even these decisions.

We shall deal mostly with forecasting for control, although the reader will very likely see ways of relating the various approaches to decision-making. However, in Chapter 22, we will describe briefly two non-statistical but mathematical forecasts which were the bases for decisions.

FORECASTING ACCURACY

Foretelling the future is forecasting with perfect accuracy. If perfection is impossible, how accurate should forecasting be? It should be as accurate and precise as we need for making the right decision or taking the right control action. As an example of the latter, a manufacturer will wish to produce at such a rate that he is generally able to meet the demand for his products, and has few dissatisfied customers;

but he will not wish, if the result is to incur large overhead costs, to create unnecessarily large stocks. His aim is to achieve an economic balance between customer service, and production and inventory costs. Apparently, the more accurately customer demand can be forecast, the more favorable the economic balance that can be obtained, and we will demonstrate this clearly in Chapter 22.

However, there are two effects which limit the value of accuracy. Firstly, accuracy can be expensive to achieve. If a manufacturer produces 20,000 parts (and that is a modest number), the analysis required to design the most accurate demand forecasting procedure for the individual parts would be impossibly expensive. A computer using simple and only moderately accurate forecasting procedures would be preferable.

Secondly, there are many restrictions on the precision with which a production process can be controlled. Beyond a certain level of precision in the demand forecast, the production process is incapable of responding so as to reduce costs. Increasing the sensitivity of a process, that is, the precision with which it can be controlled, may be expensive, but may be justified if demand can be forecast with corresponding accuracy.

The important ideas we have tried to relate here are that forecasting is essential for decision and control; that forecasting accuracy can be improved to the point where it does not improve control because of a lack of control sensitivity, and that forecasting accuracy is usually valuable, but can also be disproportionately expensive.

Chapter Nineteen

OPERATIONAL APPROACH TO FORECASTING

IN relating forecasting to control, we are taking an approach that is known as control engineering when applied to mechanical, electrical and hydraulic systems, and is now known as systems analysis or operational research when applied to business, economic or governmental systems.

There are several views as to what constitutes the systems analysis or operational approach. A useful one is to regard as a system a unit whose performance is predictable to a reasonable degree of precision. The analyst groups subjects together or subdivides them so as to form a number of units whose functioning he seems to understand (he may call these subsystems), and studies the interactions between them with the aim of developing such understanding here too, that finally he can combine them all together in one system whose operational characteristics he knows and whose performance he can therefore predict.

Referring to the manufacturing operation outlined in the previous chapter, the plant, the inventories, the customer demands, and the demand forecasting may be regarded as interacting subsystems. Having analysed the facilities and activities as subsystems, we considered the interactions between forecasting accuracy and the net revenue (itself a fairly complicated subsystem), especially the cost components of net revenue. We have shown how it is then possible to determine the most profitable value for forecasting accuracy.

DECISION THEORY—CLASSICAL STATISTICS

So far we have avoided defining any measure of accuracy. Using the operational approach, accuracy itself is irrelevant, and what concerns us is the relationship between forecasting error and net revenue. The analysis of this type of relationship is the subject of decision theory.

In applying decision theory to forecasting, we try to associate a cost with every possible combination of forecast and eventuality. The 'decision' variable could be production next month, and on the basis of a forecast of sales, and the stock of finished goods, a production manager would decide on his month's production. The cost of over-estimating sales, and hence overproducing, could be quite different from the cost of underestimating by the same amount. One leads to carrying excess stock and perhaps writing-off some stock; the other could result in the permanent loss of a customer, or might be no serious loss at all, depending on circumstances.*

At its most rigorous, decision theory requires that we understand the relationship between forecast values and the values actually realized, that is, the forecasting errors; and the relationship between the forecasting error and the system's aims and objectives, or loosely, its 'cost' function.

Classical statistics, instead of investigating the relationship between error and system cost, arbitrarily assumes that costs are proportional to the squared error. If f is a forecast and the value actually realized is X, then the forecast error is e, where

$$e = X - f$$

and the associated 'cost' of error is assumed to be e^2.

Usually the cost of error is not proportional to the square of the size of error, but assuming it to be so demands less knowledge of the system. Usually, in practice, only rather

* This type of situation is rigorously explored by Robert Schlaifer, *Probability and Statistics for Business Decisions, op. cit.*

limited knowledge is available, and determining the relationship as required by decision theory would be exorbitantly expensive.

The use of the squared error criterion may be rationalized as follows:

1. The true cost function is likely to increase with increasing size of error. The squared error function has this characteristic and is, at least to that extent, an approximation to the true cost function. If the errors are small, the approximation may be very satisfactory.

2. If the errors are large, it may be possible to adjust the squared error function quite simply so that it continues to be a satisfactory approximation.

3. There has been a vast amount of research in classical statistical theory during the past eighty years and this has resulted in standardization of procedures for dealing with problems in which the squared error function is the cost function. The decision theoretic approach, on the other hand, usually requires developing a special procedure for each problem.

Figure 1 shows a simple and common type of cost function (the solid line) and the squared error function (dotted line). The true cost function is for a production and inventory control system: a large negative error in forecasting demand (overestimating) results in increased unit costs associated with unneeded overtime working, and costs of capital for producing and storing unneeded inventory; large positive errors result in lost business through inability to meet all orders quickly. The unit costs are different in the two cases. For small errors, the costs derived from the squared error function are often not very different from the true costs.

ELEMENTARY STATISTICAL CONCEPTS

Having noted the weaknesses of the squared error cost measure we will admit that it is extremely useful and will

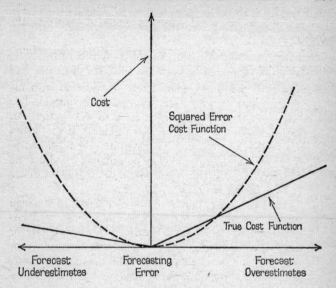

Figure 1. True and Approximate Costs Of Error

now adopt it. To begin, we shall introduce two statistical terms.

Forecasting error has already been defined as $e = X-f$. *Standard error* is a measure of the *size* of the error that tends to occur, and is usually computed as the *root mean square error*. In very many forecasting applications, errors of size greater than twice the standard deviation occur with a frequency of only one in twenty, or five per cent.

Suppose we are forecasting weekly sales of coffee and X is the quantity that will actually be sold next week. We cannot know the value of X at present, but we do know the forecast value of f. At the end of next week, we shall determine X and the forecasting error $e = X-f$.

For notational convenience, let us call the present week Week t instead of, say, the week of January 12th. We shall refer to next week as Week $t+1$, and last week as Week $t-1$. Seven days from now Week t will refer to the week of

January 19th. Our convention will be to measure time from the present increasing into the future, decreasing into the past.

Last week we sold X_{t-1} lbs. of coffee and had previously forecast sales of f_{t-1}. (Perhaps we sold 117 lbs. and had forecast 125 lbs.) The error is

$$e_{t-1} = X_{t-1} - f_{t-1} = 117 - 125 = -8 \text{ lbs.}$$

We shall be able to compute this week's error at the end of this week. Thus, if we have kept records for the past 103 weeks, we shall be able to compute e_t, e_{t-1}, e_{t-2}, e_{t-3}, ..., e_{t-103}. The *standard error*, denoted S, is computed.*

$$S = \sqrt{\frac{1}{104} \sum_{j=0}^{103} e_{t-j}^2} \quad \text{(see footnote†)}$$

In general, if our records cover N periods in the past and the current period, then we can calculate S as

$$S = \sqrt{\frac{1}{N+1} \sum_{j=0}^{N} e_{t-j}^2}$$

If we calculated S for the coffee sales forecasting procedure and found it to be, say, 15, then we would expect the forecasting error to be less than 15 lbs. in 68 weeks out of 100, and less than 30 lbs. in 95 weeks out of 100. We would not expect errors as great as 45 lbs. more often than once in four years *on average*, although certainly a particular four-year period might show two or more weeks when errors of this magnitude occurred, or there might be no such occurrences.

Very often when we graph the frequencies of occurrence of errors of various sizes, we find that they follow the curve in Figure 2 quite closely. This curve is a mathematical

---

* We shall not draw the important distinction between *standard error* and *root mean square deviation*.

† The symbol $\frac{1}{104} \sum_{j=0}^{104} e_{t-j}^2$ means that the values e_{t-j}^2 are summed for all the integer values of j from 0 to 103. t represents the current week, and when $j = 2$, e_{t-j} is e_{t-2}, the error from the week before last.

function known as the normal distribution density function, and errors whose frequency distribution closely matches this function, like those anticipated in the above example, are called *unbiased normally distributed*.* The axis shows the frequencies in which errors of all values are likely to occur. The errors are measured in multiples of the standard deviation.

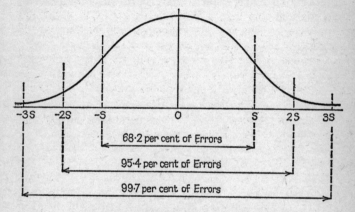

S denotes the standard error. 68·2 per cent of normally distributed errors differ from zero by not more than the standard error, 95·4 per cent by not more than twice the standard error, and 99·7 per cent by not more than three times the standard error.

Figure 2. Frequency Distribution of Errors

Without some understanding of the size of error that is likely, a forecast has no value; but often if it is not stated, the error distribution is implicit in the forecast. When a radio station announces a forecast high temperature for the day of 60°F, I would not fault the meteorologist if the

* It should be clear from the symmetry of the function that positive and negative errors of this type occur with equal frequency: there is no tendency toward one or the other, and therefore the distribution is said to be unbiased.

high were between 58° and 62°. I would not be very critical if it were between 56° and 58°, or between 62° and 64°. If the maximum were as low as 54° or as high as 66°, I would probably regard the forecast as 'wrong'. If you agree with these remarks, then, like me, you associate a standard error of approximately two degrees with forecast daily temperatures. It is not always necessary, therefore, for the forecaster to make explicit reference to the forecast error distribution.

Chapter Twenty

APPROACHES TO FORECASTING

FORECASTING MODELS — FORMAL AND STRUCTURAL

REALITY is immensely complicated, and the situations we study seem capable of many interpretations. A model is an interpretation, a simplified and incomplete expression of reality. The expression may be in terms of a set of ideas such as physics, biology, economics; and may be expressed in language or in another symbolic form such as mathematics.

The models we are to be concerned with are forecasting models; that is, interpretations of reality that apparently enable us to predict with a certain level of accuracy. Forecasting technique is the design and selection of forecasting models and their use.

Before going more deeply into forecasting technique, we shall define a few convenient terms. We shall describe as a *time series* a sequence of chronologically ordered numbers $\ldots, X_{t-1}, X_t, X_{t+1}, \ldots \ldots$, representing a quantity whose value is a function of time (i.e. subject to change from one time of observation to another). We shall begin to use *model* specifically to describe mathematically a set of assumptions on the characteristics of a time series; and the term *procedure* will be applied to a method for estimating or forecasting a value of the forecast variable.

Statistical forecasting models may be classified as *formal* or *structural*, reflecting two entirely different approaches to forecasting. The approach to formulating a formal model is to regard the forecast variable (or group of variables) as tending to follow a preselected path through time, but subject to random influences that continually deflect it from the path. What path the variable tends to follow is to be inferred from its trail. Thus, mid-day temperature might be seen as following an annual cycle from which it varies under the influence of random short term effects.

In formulating structural models, the forecast variable or set of variables is related by appropriate theory to other variables which measure the conditions of its 'environment'. (The appropriate theory may be derived from economics, sociology, or another body of knowledge.) Forecasting the variable then entails forecasting the environment. Ideally, the environment could be accurately forecast, but usually it cannot, and the problem becomes one of developing structural and formal models for forecasting the elements of the environment. Usually, however, the forecast variable may be more accurately and confidently forecast in this way than by a formal method. Certainly, some elements of the environment have been forecast very accurately in the past; and one in particular, population, has a very strong influence on many economic and business variables.*

In many countries, the number of the present inhabitants who will be alive in 15, 20, and 25 years is predictable with great confidence. Of course, this does not determine the future population. Migration is important in some areas and the migration rates at any time appear to be dependent on a combination of sociological and economic characteristics of the region or country of origin and the possible destinations of all potential migrants.

Fertility rates have their more important bearing on long-range forecasts. In many areas, most of the inhabitants 25 years from now may not yet have been born, and how many will be born is very uncertain. Birth rates are presently in a state of flux.

There are many excellent forecasting models, especially in the areas of business and economics. These are usually

* This is sometimes referred to as direct and indirect forecasting. Direct forecasting corresponds to the formal forecast where one forecasts the variable directly from its own previous pattern of fluctuations. Indirect forecasting corresponds to structural forecasting where one forecasts some other characteristic to which the variable is related and then one interprets this forecast into terms of the original variable.

thought of as structural, but, in fact, they seem to be formal-structural combinations of the type described above.

The most desirable forecasting model is derived structurally and then found to perform well. The structural derivation is some assurance that the model's future performance will be somewhat like past performance, and it thus adds a great deal of weight to the performance evaluation. It implies an understanding of the forces determining the value of the forecast variable, and is in accord with the classical idea of *scientific method*.

This assurance is important because we never know with certainty that a forecast will be accurate. A forecasting method may have seemed accurate for a very long time and still may fail in the future.* We have to recognize this, but

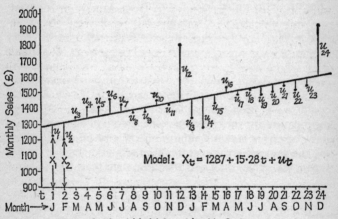

Figure 3 Trend Model for a Monthly Series

Model: $X_t = 1287 + 15 \cdot 28t + u_t$

* This is the root of forecasting accuracy. One can always be inaccurate because of chance variations but the closer we get to understanding the interrelationships of the system then the better will the forecasting process become. Hence 'good' forecasting may be separated from accurate forecasts (which may be based on unsound methods) though in the long run the sound methods will produce the more accurate forecasts because they deal with random variations more effectively. The same point is made by Hal Bierman, page 51.

we still must attempt to evaluate the model before recommending decisions based on it.

To illustrate, we shall consider the graph of monthly sales shown in Figure 3. It shows that over a two-year period, there was a steady upward trend in sales, and that from month to month, sales deviated from the trend values by varying small 'random' amounts. A formal model representing these observations is described by the following equation:

$$X_t = A + Bt + u_t$$

Time t is here measured from the first month shown. The increasing trend is at a rate of £15·28 per month and this is the value of B. The random deviations from trend are represented by the quantities u_1, u_2, ... etc., and monthly sales are represented by the quantities X_1, X_2, ...

The values chosen for A and B were determined by the least squares regression technique which selects those values that minimize the sum of squared deviations $\sum_{t=0}^{T} u_t^2$. The regression technique will be discussed in more detail later, but it should be noticed that it is not the only way A and B could have been computed or otherwise selected. The justification for the criterion of least sum of squared deviations or errors is that it minimizes the cost of error, assuming the squared error cost function. An additional property is that the values of A and B will be such that

$$\sum_{t=0}^{T} u_t = 0$$

Comparing the trend line and the actually recorded sales in Figure 3, it may occur to the reader that the difference between them each week is apparently not wholly random. The difference represents u_t, and it appears that there may be a relationship between u_t and u_{t-1}. The deviation in any week tends to be similar to the deviations in the immediately preceding and immediately following weeks. Indeed, the deviations appear to follow an annual cycle. We could elaborate on the model so as to take some account of an annual cycle thus:

$$X_t = A + Bt + C.\text{sine}\frac{2\pi}{12}t + D.\text{cosine}\frac{2\pi}{12}t + u_t$$

The model would now include the first harmonic of an annual cycle.

We could use the regression technique to compute A, B, C, and D, and we should certainly find that the new model fits the data better than the simple trend model. But we must ask what value this analysis has. Can we expect the trend B to continue into the next year? Will the same seasonal pattern continue?

We have not considered what the data actually represent – a business and economic phenomenon.* This has been a purely technical discussion of the series of quantities X_1, X_2, ... X_{24}. We have however, referred to an apparent cycle as an annual cycle, and our understanding of the business environment allows us to accept a theory of seasonal sales fluctuations.

The trouble with the formal approach is that formal interpretations are too readily accepted. One remarkable case was the heavy demand for September deliveries of a speciality product experienced by a large American pharmaceutical manufacturer. Scheduling production capacity to meet this peak demand was regarded as a necessary and unavoidable expense until an operations analyst decided that a consumer demand theory that had been accepted by management for many years was implausible. When the sales staff were questioned, they explained that in late July and August, the salesmen encouraged retailers to place large orders for September. This resulted in the salesmen receiving large commissions in August which financed their Labor

---

* It is not unknown for mathematicians to overlook that they are dealing with real-life situations upon which the business manager has much experience. The point also explains why managers are often suspicious of the mathematicians' findings which they dub as number-manipulations.

Day vacations (early September). As an inducement to the retailers, the salesmen offered special discounts on goods having unusually big margins. In fact, this practice was so well established that the company made a custom of organizing special sales promotions to support it.

The net result was a disruption of production so as to produce additional unneeded inventories in the retail shops, and the costs of these inventories reduced the annual company profit and salesmen's commissions. When all this was pointed out, the general manager eliminated the seasonal peak by means of a simple directive. This actual case illustrates the point that implicit in every formal forecasting procedure is a set of assumptions about the nature of the series of forecast variables. It is worth determining what these assumptions are, and considering their validity; for where unreasonable assumptions are implied, satisfactory forecasts should not be expected.*

* The point sounds trite and obvious. Nevertheless it is truly remarkable how frequently the error occurs in all levels of government, business and industry. Probably the most potent cause of error is failure to define the right problem – which immediately invalidates many of the key assumptions. See William Morris, page 25.

Chapter Twenty-one

STATISTICAL TECHNIQUES OF FORECASTING

THE previous sections have considered the ideas on which the mathematical-statistical approach to forecasting is based. We can sum it up quickly as follows: the approach taken is to attempt to represent a complicated process in a much simpler mathematical model; forecasting accuracy is an evaluation of the success of the attempt.

What we shall now consider is the means of producing forecasts using models. Most techniques can be thought of as having two functions. The first is to relate the model to the specific time series being forecast. This is most easily explained by reference again to the simple trend model:

$$X_t = A + Bt + u_t$$

This model might be the basis for forecasting, say, electric power consumption in a rural county; or for forecasting animal feed requirements for a predominantly urban county. Representing electric power consumption by P and feed requirements by F, we have:

$$P_t = Q + Rt + v_t$$
$$F_t = G + Ht + w_t$$

Apparently the same model is proposed for two quite different forecasts, but we do not assume that $Q = G$, $R = H$, and $v_t = w_t$. In fact, R, the rural power consumption trend could be a positive number, and H, the trend in feed requirements could be negative (decreasing requirements). Q and R, and G and H are *parameters* of the model, and their values must be estimated. Usually, especially with formal models, the estimation consists of fitting the model to the time series being forecast, the series $[P_t]$ and $[F_t]$ respectively.

When we estimate parameters we should try to learn how good the estimates are, as an indication of the confidence we may place in the forecasts dependent upon them. In the case of the trend model, we can determine the sensitivity of the fit to small errors in estimating A and B (or Q and R, etc.); and more importantly we can estimate to what extent A and B explain X_t, and the extent to which X_t is influenced by the random variable u_t. As we saw in Chapter 20, examining the fit of the model to the data can indicate the presence of explainable structure in a supposedly random series, and sometimes lead to development of a better model.

FORECASTING PROCEDURES

The second function of forecasting technique is actually to produce forecasts. The way in which this should be done depends upon the use to be made of the forecasts.

Referring again to the feed requirements model: suppose we are deciding on whether to start a feed supply business in a certain county, and intend basing the decision in part on a ten-year cash flow projection of the county's feed requirements. We could estimate G and H from past annual requirements, possibly placing most weight on recent data, and forecast by means of the equation

$$F_t = G + Ht$$

The forecasting procedure in this case bears a very obvious relationship to the model. The only difference, in fact, is that in forecasting we assume that w_t will equal zero. This assumption, by the way, has some validity, if in fitting the model we use an estimating technique that selects G and H so that the sum Σw_t, and thus the average $\bar{w}_t$ for the fitted data is approximately zero. An important technique having this property is called *multiple regression*.

If the value of G were estimated at 10,000 tons and H had been estimated at -200 tons per year, the forecast for the fifth year would be $F_5 = 10,000 - 200 \times 5 = 9,000$ tons.

Now supposing we are already supplying feed in this county and wish to make new forecasts each year. One way to do this would be to follow the same procedure as before, that is, use the values $G = 10,000$, and $H = -200$. However, each year, additional data becomes available and it is advisable to use them in forecasting the following year's feed requirements. For one thing, we may become aware of new factors influencing the requirements. Furthermore, we *know* that the model does not properly represent all the factors we are already aware of (because no model ever does), and by incorporating the most recent data in our procedure, we hope to continually adjust G and H so as to take these effects into account.

We might go beyond annually re-estimating G and H: we could even re-study the county requirements each year and develop structural models as our understanding of the origins of feed requirements improves. However, this is not practicable if feed requirements is only one of a great many time series that must be forecast. In this situation, we have to economize in the amount of record keeping and data analysis demanded by the forecasting procedure, and if possible we should provide for monitoring the forecasting performance routinely.

These considerations have led to the widespread use of two closely related types of forecasting technique – *auto-regressive* and *adaptive* forecasting.

REGRESSION

The most generally useful estimating technique for statistical forecasting is regression. We shall consider its application to estimating means and trends, and later we shall introduce other estimating applications of the technique.

First a warning: we must emphasize that very misleading results may be obtained from attempts to use regression for identifying relationships. Its proper use is estimating the parameters of relationships proposed *a priori*. The simple trend model is:

$$X_t = A + Bt + u_t$$

The random variable u_t represents the error in the relationship between the model and the recorded data. We shall estimate A and B using past records. The data are in Table 1.

TABLE 1

Time Series and Simple Trends

Year	Time(t)	X_t (actual)	X_t (Fig. 4a)	X_t (Fig. 4b) Regression
1958	−10	101	97	102
1959	−9	108	102	105
1960	−8	122	107	109
1961	−7	113	112	113
1962	−6	118	117	116
1963	−5	122	122	119
1964	−4	120	126	123
1965	−3	124	131	127
1966	−2	128	136	130
1967	−1	141	141	134

$$\Sigma t = -55$$
$$\Sigma X_t = 1197$$
$$\Sigma t^2 = 385$$
$$\Sigma t X_t = -6316$$

The time series $\{X_t\}$ is plotted in Figure 4(a). The dotted line shown is only one of an infinite number of possible trend lines which could be drawn, each line being distinguished from the others by its values for A and B. The deviation of the trend line from each data point is shown as u_{-4}, u_{-3}, ... etc. The same data are plotted again in Figure 4(b), this time with the trend model determined by

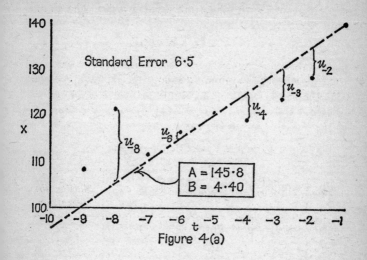

Figure 4(a)

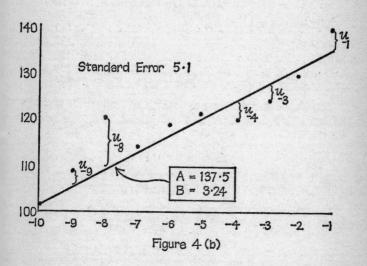

Figure 4(b)

least squares regression. The least squares model corresponds to that trend line for which the sum of the squares

$$S = u_{-10}^2 + u_{-9}^2 + \ldots + u_{-1}^2 \text{ (written } S = \sum_{t=-10}^{-1} u_t^2) \text{ is}$$

least.

At time t (where t could be any of the times from -10 to -1) the actual value of X_t is that shown in the table and plotted in the graphs. (Thus X_{-3} is 124). However, according to the model $X_t = A + Bt + u_t$.

Therefore, $u_t = X_t - (A + Bt)$
$$= X_t - A - Bt$$

For example, when t is -3

$$u_{-3} = 124 - A + 3B$$

The square of deviation u_t is:

$$u_t^2 = (X_t - A - Bt)^2$$
$$= X_t^2 - 2AX_t - 2BtX_t + 2ABt + A^2 + B^2t^2$$

The sum of squares S is:

$$S = \sum_{t=-10}^{-1} u_t^2$$

$$= \Sigma X_t^2 - 2A\Sigma X_t - 2B\Sigma t X_t + 2AB\Sigma t + \Sigma A^2 + B^2 \Sigma t^2.$$

S depends on the choice of values for A and B. Differential calculus can show that S is minimized when the partial derivatives $\partial S/\partial A$ and $\partial S/\partial B$ are both, simultaneously, equal to zero.

$$\partial S/\partial A = 0 = -2\Sigma X_t + 2B\Sigma t + 2\Sigma A$$
$$\partial S/\partial B = 0 = -2\Sigma t X_t + 2A\Sigma t + 2B\Sigma t^2$$

We now have two independent equations in two unknowns, A and B which can be solved give

$$A = \frac{(\Sigma X_t)(\Sigma t^2) - (\Sigma t)(\Sigma t X_t)}{N\Sigma t^2 - (\Sigma t)^2}$$

and

$$B = \frac{N\Sigma t X_t - (\Sigma t)(\Sigma X_t)}{N\Sigma t^2 - (\Sigma t)^2}$$

where N is the number of data points. For our data, N is 10, and the other quantities required for these formulae have been computed and are recorded in Table 1. Therefore,

$$A = \frac{1197 \times 385 - (-55)(-6316)}{10 \times 385 - (-55)^2} = 137 \cdot 5$$

and,

$$B = \frac{10 \times (-6316) - (-55) \times 1197}{10 \times 385 - (-55)^2} = 3 \cdot 24$$

The trend line with $A = 137 \cdot 5$ and $B = 3 \cdot 24$ is shown in Figure 4(b). The values of X given by each of the trend lines are compared with the true values of X in Table 1.

Our aim here has been to present the notion of regression quickly, and in using a particular example we have sacrificed a great deal of the method's general applicability. Later, we shall try to rectify this fault to some extent when we present multivariate regression. But even here, we wish to point out that regression is not limited to time series applications, and the mathematics would apply just as well if X were a function of a variable other than time. For example, the demand for a financial newspaper in various cities might be modelled by the equation $Y_k = l + m V_k + w_k$, where Y_k is demand in city k, V_k is population of males in city k earning above £2,000 per annum, and w_k is a random deviation. Regression could be used for estimating the parameters l and m.

Before the digression, we had used regression to fit a trend model to actual data. All we know about the true values of X supports the trend model but only as an approximate representation of the past relationship between X and t. We assume without justification that the model is a representation of the future relationship, too.

Even with this assumption, we do not know what value u_5 will have, nor the value of any other u_k that is a future deviation from the trend. However, as we mentioned earlier, it is a property of the least square method that the average of $u_{-10}, u_{-9}, \ldots, u_{-1}$, is zero; we identify future deviations with forecasting error, saying $u_t = e_t$, and assume that the average error will be zero. We even go so far as to justify the supposition that zero is, in a certain sense, the *expected* value for $e_t = X_t - f_t$.

Recall that the model is $X_t = A + Bt + u_t$. If we expect $e_t = u_t$ to be zero on average, then it is natural to use as a predictor

$$f_t = A + Bt$$

where A and B have the values calculated before by least squares regression.

Note how the model would behave if X_t were quite independent of time. There would be no trend, the value of B would be zero, and the model would reduce to $X_t = A + u_t$. X would be approximately constant, and A would be what is called the *mean* of X. The least squares estimate of A would be the *average* value of X. Because of this feature of its construction, the model is properly called a *mean and trend model*.

AUTOREGRESSIVE FORECASTING

Autoregressive forecasting procedures estimated future values of a variable by weighting together its own past values.

If $X_t = A + u_t$, then an estimate of A can be a forecast of X, u having an expected value of zero, as before. Brown ([1], p. 97)* describes this model using the concept of a locally constant process, one in which A varies slowly in time over short periods of time; between points which are close together in time A may be regarded as a constant.

* References at end of text.

Suppose we use as an estimate for A the average of the k previous values of X.

$$\text{Estimate } (A) = \frac{1}{k}[X_{t-k}+X_{t-k+1}+ \ldots +X_{t-1}] = \frac{1}{k}\sum_{i=1}^{k} X_{t-i}$$

Then for a forecasting procedure we may use:

$$f_{t+1} = \frac{1}{k}\sum_{i=1}^{k} X_{t-}$$

The forecasting procedure is to apply the factor $\frac{1}{k}$ to the past k values of the forecast variable, and add together the products.

With this model there is a problem in estimating A as an average of the previous k values of X. If k is large, then at time $t-k$, the value of A may have been quite different from the present value. On the other hand, if we choose a small value for k, our estimates of the value of A may fluctuate from one period to the next much more than does the true value of A.

An attempt to deal with the problem employs the exponentially weighted moving average.* This is a procedure using all past values of X to estimate A, but placing the greater weight on more recent values. In the following formula α is a positive number between zero and one, and β is the difference between α and one.

$$0 < \alpha < 1$$
$$\beta = 1 - \alpha$$
$$f_{t+1} = \text{Est}(A) = \alpha X_t + \alpha\beta X_{t-1} + \alpha\beta^2 X_{t-2} + \alpha\beta^3 X_{t-3} + \ldots$$
$$+ \ldots + \alpha\beta^k X_{t-k} + \ldots$$

If a large value (close to one) is chosen for α, then β is small (close to zero), $\alpha\beta$ is small, $\alpha\beta^2$ is very small; and thus by far the greatest weight is placed on X_t. However, if α is small, β is large (close to one), but $\alpha\beta$ and $\alpha\beta^2$ are not much smaller

* This technique has been dealt in a non-mathematical way by Ray Cuninghame-Green, ch. 15.

than α, and the moving average weights are placed almost evenly over a large number of X values. If A is regarded as quite stable, a small value should be chosen for α; but if A is considered volatile, α would be made larger. This procedure is called exponential smoothing. It smoothes the data by means of an infinite exponentially weighted autoregression.

ADAPTIVE FORECASTING

The idea behind adaptive forecasting is that if a large change in the value of the 'constant' A had just occurred, this would have caused a large forecasting error, and this error can now be used to adjust the estimate of A in producing the next forecast. Another way of expressing the idea is that adaptive forecasting 'learns from its mistakes'. According to this idea, a good forecast of X_{t+1} (or estimate of A) is the forecast of X_t made earlier, adjusted for the forecasting error, thus:

$$f_{t+1} = f_t + a.e_t$$

To illustrate, if f_t had been a perfect forecast of X_t, then e_t would be zero and f_{t+1} would be equal to f_t. However, if the forecasting error is $e_t = X_t - f_t$, and f_t badly underestimated X_t, then e_t would be large, and a positive adjustment to f_t would be required in forecasting X_{t+1}. This example shows that a must be a positive number. It suggests also that a should be smaller than $1 \cdot 0$, since otherwise the procedure will over-adjust resulting in unstable forecasting performance.

The adaptive forecasting equation can be written with e_t replaced by $X_t - f_t$:

$$\begin{aligned} f_{t+1} &= f_t + a.e_t \\ &= f_t + a.(X_t - f_t) \\ &= aX_t + f_t - af_t \\ &= aX_t + (1-a)f_t \end{aligned}$$

Of course, f_t was obtained in a similar manner to f_{t+1}; therefore

$$f_t = aX_{t-1} + (1-a)f_{t-1}$$

and using this equation to replace f_t in equation (*), we obtain

$$f_{t+1} = aX_t + (1-a)[aX_{t-1} + (1-a)f_{t-1}]$$
$$= aX_t + a(1-a)X_{t-1} + (1-a)^2 f_{t-1}$$

Replacing f_{t-1} in the same way:

$$f_{t+1} = aX_t + a(1-a)X_{t-1} + a(1-a)^2 X_{t-2} + (1-a)^3 f_{t-2}$$

Continuing this process indefinitely, and writing b for the expression $(1-a)$, we obtain

$$f_{t+1} = aX_t + abX_{t-1} + ab^2 X_{t-2} + \ldots + ab^k X_{t-k} + \ldots$$

If we replace a with α and b with β we see that this is precisely the same as the exponential smoothing equation on page 179. Therefore we may expect forecasts produced by exponential smoothing to be the same as forecasts by this type of adaptive forecasting.

There are other types of autoregressional and adaptive forecasting methods corresponding to more complicated time series models. They will not be discussed here, but the theory and several examples are described in (2) and (3).

THE IMPLICIT MODEL

The idea of a locally constant time series is represented by the following model:

$$X_t = A_t$$
$$A_t = A_{t-1} + u_t$$

The 'constant' A has the value A_t in period t, which is equal to the value it had in the previous period modified by a random disturbance u_t. If the standard deviation of u is S_u, then u_t, will be between $-2S_u$ and $+2S_u$, roughly 19

times out of 20 (assuming u to be normally distributed).
A is usually within $2S_u$ of its previous value, but often it will
change by more than this amount over a few periods. Table
2 shows a series like X_t generated artificially using a table
of random variables. Figure 5 shows a graph of this series.
The series is 'constant' about the value 22·9 for six periods
and at about the value 20·7 for seven periods; for four
periods it has values around 16·8.

TABLE 2

Artificially Constructed Locally Constant Series

$$X_t = A_t$$
$$A_t = A_{t-1} + U_t$$

$\{U_t\}$ is normally distributed with expected value zero, and
standard deviation 1·0

t	U_t	A_{t-1}	$X_t = A_t$ $A_t = A_{t-1}+U_t$	t	U_t	A_{t-1}	X_t
40	·5	20·0	20·5	54	−·3	17·0	16·7
41	·1	20·5	20·6	55	·2	16·7	16·9
42	2·5	20·6	23·1	56	·8	16·9	17·7
43	−·3	23·1	22·8	57	·2	17·7	17·9
44	−·1	22·8	22·7	58	−·3	17·9	17·6
45	·3	22·7	23·0	59	1·6	17·6	19·2
46	−·3	23·0	22·7	60	1·1	19·2	20·3
47	·1	22·7	22·8	61	·4	20·3	20·7
48	−2·5	22·8	20·3	62	−·5	20·7	20·2
49	−·5	20·3	19·8	63	1·0	20·2	21·2
50	−1·9	19·8	17·9	64	−·5	21·2	20·7
51	·5	17·9	18·4	65	·2	20·7	20·9
52	−1·6	18·4	16·8	66	−·2	20·9	20·7
53	·2	16·8	17·0				

There is no better least squares method than exponential smoothing (or the equivalent adaptive forecasting procedure) for forecasting series of this type. The dotted line in Figure 5 connects adaptively forecast points, and the computation of the forecasts is shown in Table 3. In many applications a smoothing constant value of from ·1 to ·3 performs well, and generally the success of the method is not dependent on

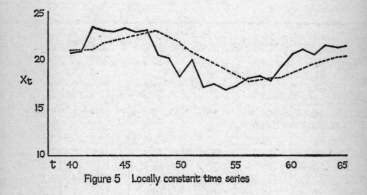

Figure 5   Locally constant time series

carefully choosing this value. However, a rigorous theory exists on which the optimal value of the smoothing constant can be determined ((2), (3), and (4)).

The model is not very useful for business or economic forecasting; if it seems to represent a real series, then the series cannot be forecast with any accuracy beyond the next one or two time periods. In fact, the model is not like many real time series involving business or economic variables. It is quite 'unstable' and more closely resembles certain real series when it is 'damped'. (It is inappropriate to develop these ideas here. An intuitive interpretation of the terms 'unstable' and 'damped' will convey the notions adequately). When damped, it is sometimes suggested as a good representation of day-to-day changes in stock market prices.

TABLE 3

Simulated Adaptive Forecasting for a Locally
Constant Series

$$f_t = f_{t-1} + a(X_{t-1} - f_{t-1})$$
Smoothing Constant $a = 0.3$

t	X_{t-1}	f_{t-1}	f_t	X_t	L_t
40	20·0	20·9*	20·6	20·5	−·1
41	20·5	20·6	20·6	20·6	0
42	20·6	20·6	20·6	23·1	2·5
43	23·1	20·6	21·4	22·8	1·4
44	22·8	21·4	21·8	22·7	·9
45	22·7	21·8	22·1	23·0	·9
46	23·0	22·1	22·4	22·7	·3
47	22·7	22·4	22·5	22·8	·3
48	22·8	22·5	22·6	20·3	−2·3
49	20·3	22·6	21·9	19·8	−2·1
50	19·8	21·9	21·3	17·9	−4·0
51	17·9	21·3	20·1	18·4	−1·7
52	18·4	20·1	19·6	16·8	−2·8
53	16·8	19·6	18·8	17·0	−1·8
54	17·0	18·8	18·3	16·7	−1·6
55	16·7	18·3	17·8	16·9	−·9
56	16·9	17·8	17·5	17·7	·2
57	17·7	17·5	17·6	17·9	·3
58	17·9	17·6	17·7	17·6	−·1
59	17·6	17·7	17·7	19·2	1·5
60	19·2	17·7	18·2	20·3	2·1
61	20·3	18·2	18·8	20·7	1·9
62	20·7	18·8	19·4	20·2	·8
63	20·2	19·4	19·6	21·2	1·6
64	21·2	19·6	20·1	20·7	·6
65	20·7	20·1	20·3	20·9	·3
66	20·9	20·3	20·4	20·7	·3

* Generated from earlier data, not shown.

We can be misled by the *appearance* of trends in Figure 5, and stock market amateurs are misled in the same way every day. Because of the way in which we constructed the series we are certain that any apparently consistent movement, up or down, a trend, is entirely accidental.

A more useful model is obtained by extending the locally constant model to include a *changing trend*. In this model, changes in the value of the series are, to an extent, systematic, and only partly random. If the series has been increasing, then there is a tendency for it to continue increasing. It can change direction and decrease, but, unlike the locally constant model, it tends to maintain its current direction.

$$X_t = A_t + u_t$$
$$A_t = A_{t-1} + B_t$$
$$B_t = B_{t-1} + v_t$$

Now there are two random disturbances, u and v. The trend value B in any period is the previous period's value modified by the disturbance v (which can be positive or negative). The 'constant' term A is no longer constant in any sense, but changes from one period to the next by the current value of the trend.

In practice, this probably is the simplest useful statistical model for a volatile series. Suitably damped, it has validity in many cases, and can be forecast by variants of the exponential smoothing or adaptive forecasting procedures as before.

The procedure proposed by Brown is known as *double exponential smoothing* ([1], p. 138), but he applies it in its adaptive forecasting form. The first step in the procedure is to apply the adaptive formula as in the locally constant model.

$$f_{t+1} = f_t + a(X_t - f_t)$$

The next step is to 'smoothe' this 'forecast' using a similar procedure

$$f'_{t+1} = f'_t + a(f_t - f'_t)$$

Brown takes as estimates of A and B

$$\text{Est.} (A) = 2f_{t+1} - f'_{t+1}$$

$$\text{Est.} (B) = \frac{a}{b}(f_{t+1} - f'_{t+1})$$

and constructs forecasts for k periods ahead from the equation

$$\text{Est.} (X_{t+k}) = \text{Est.} (A_t) + k.\text{Est.} (B_t)$$

This approach is convenient, but it is not usually the most accurate, even when the model is very appropriate. A more satisfactory procedure for damped models of the type under discussion was developed by N. Wiener [5]. The theory and a method of application are described in [2] (page 97) and in [3]. Briefly stated, it amounts to converting the series $\{X_t\}$ to a series $\{Y_t\}$ having the special characteristics that an adaptive forecasting procedure applied to Y results in the least squared error forecast of Y. The forecast of Y may then be converted to a forecast of X. Application of this method to the changing trend model is discussed in [6] and [4], and in [3].

A more sophisticated model of this sort has been applied to forecasting certain seasonal series. The model, described more fully in [3], supposes the current value of a series of monthly data to depend on three components: the mean, the trend, and the month itself. The monthly or 'seasonal' effect is similar to the changing trend effect described above except that it is specific to a particular month, and changes from year to year. Thus, if there were an increasing trend in December sales, the model and the associated forecasting procedure would represent this by considering the sales in the previous two Decembers, and simultaneously account for any recent short term trend affecting sales in the October and November.

This model was designed for forecasting monthly employment series in the United States. In the following equations there are three kinds of random disturbance, u, v, and w, all having different standard deviations. A_t and B_t have the same meanings as in the changing trend model. A damping constant ρ is also shown.

M_t is the current level of the monthly component and is not related at all to M_{t-1}, the monthly component for the previous month, but is related to M_{t-12}, the component for the same month one year earlier. The relationship involves the *change* in monthly component m_t which has the value it held twelve months earlier, modified by a random disturbance. The model is

$$X_t = A_t + M_t + u_t$$
$$A_t = \rho A_{t-1} + B_t$$
$$B_t = \rho B_{t-1} + v_t$$
$$M_t = M_{t-12} + m_t$$
$$m_t = m_{t-12} + w_t$$

Developing a prediction procedure for this model was quite difficult and involved using spectral analysis as a method of estimating the damping factor and two other constants. The spectrum of a time series is a function that characterizes the interrelationship between the values of the series. The estimation technique consisted of determining, theoretically, the type of spectrum which should be associated with the series if it were indeed generated by the model, and comparing it with an observed spectrum, that is, a spectrum derived from the actual monthly employment data. The theoretical spectrum was then adjusted by varying the three constants until it closely matched the observed spectrum. The resulting theoretical and the observed spectra are shown in Figure 6. The fact that very close correspondence was achieved was taken as evidence of the model's validity.

The values of the constants that resulted in the best match between the spectra were used in converting the series $\{X_t\}$ to a series $\{Y_t\}$, adaptively forecasting $\{Y_t\}$, and converting the forecasts of Y into forecasts of X. Figures 7a, b, and c show the computer-simulated application of the method to forecasting monthly employment of males aged 14–19.* In

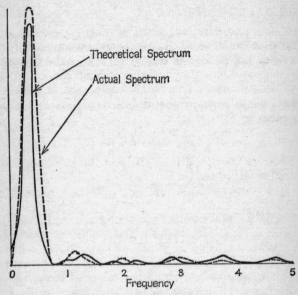

Figure 6   Seasonal Model

Figure 7a, the dotted line shows a series of monthly employment forecasts made on the basis of data available at the end of the previous month. Thus, the forecast for April 1954, was calculated on the basis of actual employment data up to March 1954. As one would expect, forecasts made one month ahead tend to be more accurate than those

* During this study very many theoretical spectra were computed and there were several simulated tests of the forecasting procedure. It was a great convenience to have these two types of results automatically drawn on graph paper by the computer, as well as reported in tabular form. Figure 7 was in fact originally drafted by a computer-controlled machine.

made four or fifteen months ahead. Four-month forecasts are shown in Figure 7b, and Figure 7c shows fifteen-month forecasts.

MULTIPLE REGRESSION

We have considered two types of models for which regression provides an estimating technique: the time series model, in which the 'dependent' variable is indexed by time periods

$$X_t = A + Bt + u_t$$

and a model in which the dependent variable Y is indexed by cities

$$Y_k = l + mV_k + w_k$$

In each of these, the parameters of the two 'independent' variables are estimated.*

It is mathematically and conceptually straightforward

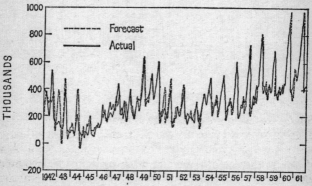

Fig 7(a) Actual and forecasted unemployment of males, aged 14-19 Forecasted one month ahead.

* The use of the words 'dependent' and 'independent' implies a causal relationship, which must be based on economic, social, or other theory. Mathematically, A is the coefficient of a quantity whose value is always 1·0, and B is the coefficient of a measure of time, and A and B are interdependent.

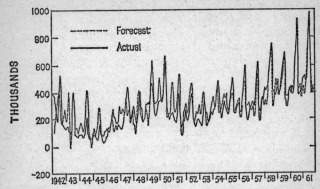

Fig 7(b) Actual and forecasted unemployment of males, aged 14-19
Forecasted four months ahead.

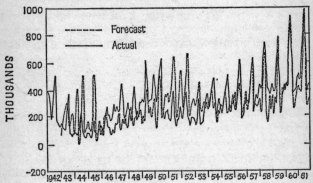

Fig 7(c) Actual and forecasted unemployment of males, aged 14-19
Forecasted fifteen months ahead.

to extend the use of regression to estimating coefficients for more than two independent variables, thus:

$$X_t = A + Bt + CY_t + DZ_t + u_t$$

where $\{Y\}$ and $\{Z\}$ are time series; and more generally:

$$X_{1,k} = a_2 X_{2,k} + a_3 X_{3,k} + \ldots + a_m X_{m,k} + u_k$$

A word of warning, however: if any two independent variables are highly *correlated* it becomes difficult to estimate the separate coefficients. This effect is known as 'multi-colinearity', and often leads to quite incorrect conclusions when regression is used in attempts to *identify* relationships rather than as a means of estimating parameters of relationships. A detailed introductory treatment of multiple regression is given in [7].

Multiple regression obviously extends regression to many types of applications although from the methodological standpoint, it is very similar to simple regression. However, there is an interesting class of models which depend on the multivariate capability of multiple regression. These use the *dummy variable* concept, which we will describe as applied to forecasting a seasonal time series.

X_t is a series of quarterly (3-monthly) data. Assume that a suitable model is

$$X_t = A + Bt + C_s + u_t$$

A, B, and u have their usual meanings (mean, trend, and random disturbance): and C_s is a seasonal variable. The magnitude of C depends on whether s is 1, 2, 3, or 4, corresponding to the four quarters of the year.

One way to estimate coefficients for this model would be to analyse each season separately, applying multiple regression first to winter data, then spring data, etc. This would result in estimates for C_1, C_2, C_3 and C_4; but it would also produce four separate estimates each for A and B. There are techniques for pooling these separate entities to provide single estimates each for A and B. However, the dummy variable technique permits producing separate estimates for C_1, C_2, C_3, C_4, and single pooled estimates for A and B in one set of multiple regression calculations.

The dummy variable technique is to replace C_s by four coefficients c_1, c_2, c_3 and c_4; and 'dummy' variables δ_1, δ_2, δ_3 and δ_4. We define δ_1 to be equal to $1 \cdot 0$ in the first quarter, and zero in the second, third, and fourth quarters, thus:

$$\delta_1 = \begin{cases} 1 \cdot 0 \text{ if } s = 1 \\ 0 \text{ if } s \neq 1 \end{cases}$$

Similarly,

$$\delta_2 = \begin{cases} 1\cdot0, & s = 2 \\ 0, & s \neq 2 \end{cases}$$

Or in general,

$$\delta_k = \begin{cases} 1\cdot0, & s = k \\ 0, & s \neq k \end{cases}$$

The equation to be estimated by regression is then

$$X_t = A + Bt + c_1\delta_1 + c_2\delta_2 + c_3\delta_3 + c_4\delta_4 + u_t$$

Chapter Twenty-two

EXAMPLES OF MATHEMATICAL AND STATISTICAL FORECASTING IN BUSINESS

A FEW forecasting applications described in other chapters were chosen for their relevance to the discussion of particular forecasting techniques. The applications described in this chapter are to illustrate the application of forecasting techniques, and to describe some special examples.

STOCK CONTROL

Stock control systems are designed to balance the requirement for ready availability of supplies against the need to limit the costs associated with inventory: rental or investment in warehouse space, salaries and wages for warehouse personnel, and the cost of capital invested in stock, facilities, maintenance, etc.

It may be obvious, but we shall repeat it anyway, that the most important reason for keeping stock is to ensure ready availability of goods. Without stocks a wholesaler's customers' orders are delayed by the amount of time needed to ship and transport goods from the manufacturer; and if a manufacturer does not maintain stocks, his customers' shipmates are delayed until the next production runs of items that have been ordered.

The role of forecasting in inventory control is to indicate when and how much to reorder, and it acts by indicating the likely requirements for items during the delivery lead time. For example, if it takes three weeks from the time an order is initiated until the goods are received and ready, then the order should be placed when there are still sufficient stocks to meet requirements for three weeks.

We shall discuss two applications of forecasting in stock control. The first deals with the importance of forecasting accuracy in stock control, and the second with an unusual forecasting model.

(1) FORECASTING ACCURACY AND STOCK CONTROL

Experience with many stock control systems has shown exponential smoothing (in the adaptive form) to be a satisfactory forecasting method for quite general use. However, some items are subject to sporadic demand or to strong seasonal variations in demand, and when exponential forecasting is used for these, the forecasting errors are large. In designing a stock control system, the extra costs for incorporating special forecasting procedures for these items should be compared with the savings to be expected as a result of the improvement in accuracy. We shall use a simplified example to indicate the value of forecasting accuracy and the incentive for applying a more accurate forecasting technique.

Figure 8 shows one year of stock level history for an item. The management has decided that an appropriate inventory policy is to ensure that for this item, there should be at least a 95% chance that it is in stock *at all times*. The system in use is to reorder when the stock falls to a point where there is sufficient remaining to ensure that there is a 95% chance of being able to meet customer orders from the shelf during the period of awaiting the new delivery. This critical stock level is calculated by forecasting *demand for the delivery lead time* and adding to that amount a safety stock to protect against forecasting errors.

The more accurate the forecasting, the smaller may the safety stock be. For the item represented in Figure 8, the safety stock is 120 units. If the standard error of forecasts could be halved, the safety stock could be reduced to 60 units, and the resulting saving could be computed by conventional cost accounting methods.

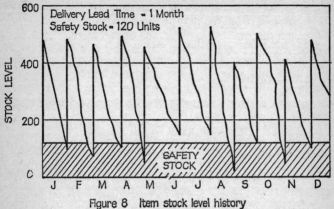

Figure 8   Item stock level history

(2) DEMAND FOR STYLE ITEMS

Most ladies' fashion houses display their entire stocks of dresses, coats, etc., in racks placed about the sales floor and available for the customers to inspect. Usually each style is ordered in a few colours and sizes, but typically the total number of each style in stock is small. There may be only one or two in each colour-size combination, and perhaps six or twelve altogether.

The size of the original order is decided by the buyer, who judges how attractive the style will be to her firm's clientele. She must not order too many in any style, for if any remain at the end of the season they have to be sold off cheaply or scrapped.

Although certain types of data are now being assembled which will assist in buying in the future, deciding on the initial order each season will likely remain a matter for the buyer's expert judgement. However, once a style is in stock it is possible to forecast demand quite well by statistical methods, and to assist the buyer in deciding how many items to reorder and when to reorder [8]. This assistance is particularly valuable because the wholesale suppliers do not stock most styles for more than a short time after the season begins.

The forecasting procedure is based on a behavioral model of demand. Very briefly, it states that for a given style, demand is proportional to the number of items on display. (Demand differs, of course, for different styles.) Thus, if the intial order were 12 items and six were sold in the first week, we would forecast that three would be sold in the second week. The times taken to sell the first two or three items constitute a good statistical indicator for estimating the rate of sale and for making the reorder decision.

This model and the associated forecasting procedure have now been incorporated in a stock control system which will be available to users of a very widely distributed line of computers.

AGRICULTURAL COMMODITY FORECASTS

For many commodities there are very lively markets. Contracts for future production are traded in much the same way as stocks and shares, and the prices fluctuate with changing opinion on what will be the future relationship between demand and supply. Experts judge the effect a late frost or summer hail will have on the size of the future harvest, and traders interpret the information relative to the demand for the crop. At present there are large stocks of frozen orange juice concentrate in the United States, but a drought has occurred which will reduce the forecast for next year's production, and prices for spot and future contracts for the next eleven months have already responded.

Because many of the factors governing demand and supply of agricultural commodities are well known, it is often possible to make good forecasts. To illustrate this we will discuss the supply of wool grown in the United States.

In the US, wool is a by-product of lamb production: sheep farmers receive about two-thirds of their income from meat, and only one-third from wool. Almost all sheep not slaughtered as lambs are ewes which are kept primarily as a source of lambs, and only incidently as a source of wool. There is virtually no market for mutton in the US, probably because the costs of producing and marketing it would place it at a price disadvantage compared with beef. Two other essential considerations are that income from wool growing has been stabilized by government action; and that on the other hand, lamb prices fluctuate widely, and income from lamb is not stabilized.

A short study of how growers and the market would be likely to react to various types of disturbance led to the formulation of a group of supply determination models. The most important effect on wool supply, reflected in all the models, was considered to be the previous year's lamb prices. Various mechanisms were suggested as affecting interaction between lamb prices and wool supply, but one that seemed particularly important was as follows: if lamb prices are high, growers will decide to take immediate advantage of the fact: they will market some lambs that otherwise would have been kept for breeding, and incidently would have contributed to the following years' wool supply. The reason this was plausible was that wool growers seemed to consider themselves to be under severe economic pressure, and it was likely, therefore, that they would make decisions on the basis of a short term forecast of conditions. If growers took a long term view, the most plausible model would anticipate increased wool supply next year resulting from expected continuance of the high current prices for lamb.

In the following equation, W_t is the supply of US wool in year t, and p_t is the average US lamb price for the year. A is a constant.

$$W_t = A + Bp_{t-1} + u_t.$$

The equation was fitted by regression, and the standard deviation was found to be 5% of the average annual wool supply. This result lends support to the model, and suggests that more careful analysis would lead to an accurate forecasting procedure.

MATHEMATICAL FORECASTING MODELS

Mathematical forecasting models is a term we use to describe quantitative forecasting models which do not depend directly on statistical analysis. Their role is usually to contribute to decision-making rather than control.

As we said earlier, forecasts are valueless without some understanding of the probable forecasting errors, and the costs of errors; and it is the analysis of estimation error that characterizes mathematical statistics. However, many decisions must be made without the benefit of data amenable to statistical analysis, and besides, it often happens that the decision problem can be described in such terms that large errors can be tolerated and very accurate forecasting is unnecessary. Sometimes, too, subjective assessments of the forecasting error can be made quite confidently once the forecasting model has been formulated. One of the values of a mathematical model is that it helps *define* the decision problem, and thus simplifies it.

This type of model is usually specially designed for a specific problem, and as a result examples are very varied and hard to classify. For this reason it is hard to select one as being especially representative and a good illustration of forecasting technique. However, they do tend to be interesting, and it is mainly for this reason that two are included. They are described in outline only.

(1) FORECASTING THE DEMAND FOR A NEW PRODUCT

A firm deciding on whether to construct a prototype machine for washing large aircraft wished to know if the potential market were sufficient to justify the investment required to develop and produce the machine.

The airlines, the potential customers, would not commit

themselves by telling the manufacturer how many machines they would purchase, if any, before seeing it in operation, and having an opportunity to consider its performance from a financial standpoint. Since direct inquiry was unsuccessful, the approach taken instead was to interview appropriate staff in major airlines and discover the place occupied by washing within their maintenance programs, the washing time and direct costs associated with the currently available washing methods, and the influence of winter weather on the choice of locations for washing. On the basis of the information obtained, those airports were identified where airlines would be likely to place washing equipment, and the number of machines required to maintain present standards of aircraft washing was estimated. On this basis, it was found that the cost of using the new equipment would be very considerably less than present washing costs, and that the minimum number likely to be required was considerably more than the manufacturer needed in order to begin to make a profit. In fact, the probable size of the market was estimated, but the key number for the manufacturer's decision was the *minimum* probable market. Only subjective assessments of probable error were used, but the decision to go ahead was made very confidently.

(2) FORECASTING CANAL TOLLS

Some time ago, a study was made to determine whether an increase in Panama Canal tolls would increase revenue, or result in such a loss of traffic that revenues would decline.

The value of the canal to shipowners is mainly in the time it saves them and the increased utilization it permits them to obtain from their ships. A model was designed to determine the value of the canal to world shipping. It reflected various types of cargoes, their origins and destinations; various types of ship, and their routeing, assuming that ship-owners will choose the route that is most advantageous to them.

By means of this model it was possible to estimate the effect on traffic of alternative canal toll schedules. The results showed that if tolls were increased revenues would at first increase; but that beyond a certain point, further increases in tolls would result in reduced revenues because of reduced traffic. Nevertheless, it was found that increasing tolls up to that level would be likely to result in a very sizeable increase in revenue.

REFERENCES

1. R. G. Brown, *Smoothing, Forecasting and Prediction* (Prentice-Hall, 1963), p. 97.

2. P. Whittle, *Prediction and Regulation* (The English Universities Press, 1963).

3. D. Couts, D. Grether, M. Nerlove, 'Forecasting Non-Stationary Economic Time Series', *Management Science*, Volume 13 (September 1966), pp. 1–21.

4. M. Nerlove, S. Wage, 'On the Optimality of Adaptive Forecasting', *Management Science*, Volume 10 (January 1964), pp. 202–224.

5. N. Wiener, *Extrapolation, Interpolation, and Smoothing of Stationary Time Series* (Wiley, 1949).

6. H. Theil, S. Wage, 'On some observations on Adaptive Forecasting', *Management Science*, Volume 10, January 1964.

7. Owen L. Davies, *Statistical Method in Research and Production* (Oliver & Boyd, 1958).

8. H. B. Wolfe, 'Forecasting Demand for Style Items', *IMR*, Volume 9, No. 2 (Winter 1968), p. 69.

Other useful books on forecasting which are not referred to in the text are:

A. Battersby, *Sales Forecasting* (Cassell, 1968).

J. V. Gregg, C. H. Hossell and J. T. Richardson, *Mathematical Trend Curves; an Aid to Forecasting* (Oliver & Boyd, 1964).

G. A. Coutie, O. L. Davies, C. H. Hossell, D. W. G. P. Millar and A. J. H. Morrell, *Short Term Forecasting* (Oliver & Boyd, 1964).

R. H. Woodward and P. L. Goldsmith, *Cumulative-Sum Techniques* (Oliver & Boyd, 1964).

Management Series

MARKETING MANAGEMENT IN ACTION 60p
Victor P. Buell. A guide to successful marketing management by a former national vice-president of the American Marketing Association.

THE AGE OF DISCONTINUITY 60p
Peter F. Drucker. The author presents numerous practical examples from Central Europe, Britain, US, and Japan.

MANAGING FOR RESULTS 40p
Peter F. Drucker. A what-to-do book for the top echelons of management.

CYBERNETICS IN MANAGEMENT 40p
F. H. George. Introduction to the ideas and methods used by cyberneticians in the running of modern business and government.

PLANNED MARKETING 35p
Ralph Glasser. A lucid introduction to mid-Atlantic marketing techniques.

FINANCE AND ACCOUNTS FOR MANAGERS 35p
Desmond Goch. A vital and comprehensive guide to the understanding of financial problems in business.

INNOVATION TO MARKETING 40p
Theodore Levitt. A brilliant exposition of original and stimulating ideas on modern approaches to marketing.

THE ESSENCE OF PRODUCTION 40p
P. H. Lowe. Explains the components, diversities and problems of production within the general framework of business management.

MANAGEMENT SERIES (cont.)

**A MANPOWER
DEVELOPMENT SYSTEM**   40p
James J. Lynch. Part 2 of *Making Manpower Effective*. Shows the need to integrate manpower forecasting, compensation planning and career development into a manpower development system.

CAREERS IN MARKETING   30p
An Institute of Marketing Review. A guide to those seeking a job in the exciting field of marketing.

SELLING AND SALESMANSHIP   30p
R. G. Magnus-Hannaford. A clear, concise and forward-looking exposition of practical principles and their application.

MARKETING   37½p
Colin McIver. Includes chapters by Gordon Wilson on the Years of Revolution and Industrial Marketing.

**EXPORTING: A Basic Guide to Selling
Abroad**   37½p
Robin Neillands and Henry Deschampneufs. Shows how smaller and medium-sized companies can effectively obtain and develop overseas markets.

**DYNAMIC BUSINESS
MANAGEMENT**   30p
Harold Norcross. A simple guide to the rudiments of successful business management.

**FINANCIAL PLANNING
AND CONTROL**   40p
R. E. Palmer & A. H. Taylor. Explains the nature of the assistance which levels of accounting can provide in the planning and control of a modern business.

MANAGEMENT SERIES (cont.)

MANAGEMENT INFORMATION –
Its Computations and Communication   45p
C. W. Smith, G. P. Mead, C. T. Wicks and
G. A. Yewdall.   Discusses Education in Busi-
ness Management, Statistics for Business,
Mathematics and Computing, Operational
Research, Communicating Numerical Data.

MANAGERS AND THEIR JOBS   35p
Rosemary Stewart. Helps managers to analyse what they can do, why they do it, and
whether they can, in fact, do it better.

THE REALITY OF MANAGEMENT   40p
Rosemary Stewart.   Compass bearings to help
the manager plot his career.

BUSINESS PLANNING   45p
D. R. Halford. An absorbing and stimulating analysis of planning in all its facets.

HOW TO WIN CUSTOMERS   45p
Heinz M. Goldmann. A leading European
sales consultant with unique experience of
British, Canadian, US and European markets
examines the sixteen areas of creative selling.

These Management Series titles are obtainable
from all good booksellers. If you have any
difficulty please send purchase price, plus 7p
postage to PO Box 11, Falmouth Cornwall.
While every effort is made to keep prices low, it
is sometimes necessary to increase prices at
short notice. PAN Books reserve the right to
show new retail prices on covers which may
differ from those advertised in the text or
elsewhere.